Heart Drums

by

Bonnie Ray

authorHOUSE™

1663 LIBERTY DRIVE, SUITE 200
BLOOMINGTON, INDIANA 47403
(800) 839-8640
WWW.AUTHORHOUSE.COM

First published by AuthorHouse 05/17/05

ISBN: 1-4208-3751-6 (sc)

Printed in the United States of America
Bloomington, Indiana

This book is printed on ccid-free paper.

Messenger

He danced and he soared in playful display
His message he delivered to me that day
Eagle of heaven sent from above
He delivered a message sent with love
Go tell it on the mountain and in the valleys below
The stories and songs from long long ago
Tell them of the bravery and blood shed
Of the road where many lay dead
Speak our heart song of forgiveness
So the truth will be known when it is read
Our legends and lore live on and on
Even though many we lost are gone
We still forever remain the first and the last
From the day Our Creator made the first cast

Foreword

Born of Irish and Cherokee parents in 1942 in Indianapolis, Indiana I have lived long enough to watch my dreams be born and live. And others I have cried a million tears over as I watched them die Writing this book is my greatest dream come true! I love sharing my life and heart with those that have walked the same road as I. So I put my heart and soul into giving this piece of my heart to the world. I'm sure there are feelings in this book you have felt at one time or another, but some how couldn't quite express them. So enjoy and share with those you love.

Many thanks, Bonnie

Dedications

I dedicate this book to my two Angels Frank and Alice Ann Pellegrino. Whom without their kind and loving encouragement this book would still be a dream.
May they always be as blessed as I am... by just knowing them.

Other Angels that have touched my heart and made me keep writing when I was ready to throw away my pen are: Maryfrances Perez, Floreann Cawley, Marie Boyd, and a special thank you to the one that opened my heart and made the pen flow forth Dr. Richard T. Brent

Welcome to my campfire
Please have a seat beside me
Listen with your heart
As yesterday echoes from the past...

Table of Contents

A Very special thank you to (CherokeeRose) for her beautiful artwork. She created the book cover and the Native American art on the poems throughout this book.

Thank you sis for the many hours you labored to create these beautiful drawings.

Chapter One
Native American Poetry
The Good Red Roads -

Code of Ethics

1. *Search for yourself, by yourself. Do not allow others to make your path for you. It is your road, and yours alone. Others may walk it with you, but no one can walk it for you.*

2. *Treat the guests in your home with much consideration. Serve them the best food, give them the best bed and treat them with espect and honor.*

3. *Do not take what is not yours. Whether from a person, a community, the wilderness or from a culture. It was not earned nor given. It is not yours. You cannot enjoy what it not yours.*

4. *Respect all things that are placed upon this Earth.*

5. *Rise with the sun to pray. Pray alone. Pray often. The Great Spirit will listen, if only you speak.*

6. *Honor other people's thoughts, wishes and words. Never interrupt another or mock or mimic them. Allow each person the right to a freedom of opinion. Respect that opinion.*

7. *Never speak of others in a bad way. The negative energy that you put out into the universe will multiply when it returns to you.*

8. *All persons make mistakes. No matter how small or how large the mistake is, it can still be forgiven.*

9. *Bad thoughts cause illness of the spirit, the mind and the body. Keep bad thoughts at bay. Practice optimism.*

10. Nature is not FOR us, it is a PART of us. Treat all natural beings as a member of your family.
11. Children are the seeds of our future. Plant love in their hearts and water them with wisdom and life's lessons. When they are grown, allow them find their own place.
12. Keep yourself balanced. Your Mental self, Spiritual Self, Emotional Self and Physical self all need to be strong, pure and healthy. Work out the body, to strengthen the mind. Grow rich in spirit to cure emotional ails.
13. Make conscious decisions as to who you will be and how you will react. Be responsible for your own actions.
14. Treat the elders as special gems - their wisdom will shine.
15. Be true to yourself first.

Heart Drums

The drums beat within my heart
I listen when they start
My soul becomes one with the drum
And my feet will dance the song
The story will unfold to some
My people they are strong
The stories of old ,are now being told
Wisdom to you does come
With the beat of the heart drum
Grandfather is talking
Listen with your heart
As you walk the ancient trails
Tales of the past as heart and soul hungers..
now feast at last
Mind pictures will unfold
Listen with your heart
As the stories be told

O'siyo Grandfather

A moment in times gone forever
The wind is stirring, my hair is blowing
gently in the wind.
As I sit here on this highest hill
I look into the valley below I
see the herd and the stallion in the lead
His tail blowing free behind him
and his mare keeping pace beside him
Mane flowing in the wind
as he races across the valley floor.
Softly I hear a whisper in my ear...
O'siyo Grandfather, I hear you
Welcome !
I know you are here beside me,
It has been awhile since last we talked
I have missed you.
Your wisdoms and the stories of old
I have longed to hear them once again
Yes they are beautiful ,,the horses below
they are free as we once were, in the long ago.
The stallion has the spirit of the fire and the
swiftness of the wind.
Also the wisdom of mother earth to
lead his herd far from the dangers to grazing
that is pure and untainted.
He too must remember the camp fires

that used to glow in the night
When our people and his kind
shared this beautiful land
The time of peace and harmony.
Soon grandfather I will join you
we will cross this land and remember
Ah yes I see ..brother eagle in the distance
He too longs for those days as well
Grandfather must you go so soon ?
I will wait for your return .....
As grandfather faded from my sight
trees stir and I felt his touch upon my brow
His words echoing in the wind..
be well my child
remember who you are.. Cherokee
Earthkeeper
As a feather drifted to land at my feet..

I Am

I am...
you me and we
All a part of The ONE
I am woman ,mother , grandmother,
giver of heart and love.
I am your daughter, sister , aunt , cousin,
I am by birth and heart Cherokee
I am proud , yet I am humble
To you ..
I will extend my hand should you stumble
Does not matter the color of your skin
if we all take the time to look within
In me you will find a true sister and a friend.
I have been called by many names.
Discrimination calls me Indian!
The Creator above calls me His child
I am Native American and I have walked upon
this earth many times before discrimination was born.
Time after time , my roots were shattered and torn.
But my heritage stands proud !
The legends and lore speak loud.
Again and again we are reborn.
I am, flesh and blood, yet I am the Spirit of yesterday
Striving towards a better tomorrow ,
as I push discrimination out of my way.
I am.. a part of the past ,the present, and the future.

I am one..yet I am many
Come take my hand and walk with me across the land
and across the sea.
Live in peace and harmony as it is meant to be.
You and I are a part of the...
I Am

Two Of Me

Upon my face you can see two of me
One is of Irish
And one is of Cherokee
Within my blood, I carry the best of both
When I hear the drums of my ancestors
there is a bagpipe that crys a sad melody
Because the two clans , both suffered
and ,fought and died in deaths comraderie
Within me I carry the blood ..
of ancients of two worlds
Proud I am ...that there is two of me
One of Irish and one of Cherokee
We are a proud people and have faced
the worlds many tradgedy
Two cultures,one heart blended in harmony
Many years ago the Cherokee reached across the sea
with an open heart and hand and answered a plea
To those that had nothing, they gave love and honesty
For they to had walked the same roads and struggled
to survive life's tragedies
From the emerald isle
my grandfather,came to wed
his bride of Cherokee
And that my friend is why you see..
two of me

Bonnie Ray

Mother's Voice

Listen and you can hear her voice
In the quiet of twilight...
Each evening she sings a song of rejoice
Hear her melody drift through the sighing leaves
As high above the Eagle watches his kingdom
And from the brook hear her laughing tease
Mother's voice soft and gentle carried by the breeze
As the sunset melts into the arms of sleep
Stars begin their twinkling delight
While the moon keeps watch all through the night
Mother's voice sings her lullabyes to us her children
Forever reassuring even in lifes fleeting flight
That birth and death are one and the same..
step into heaven

If you talk to the animals
they will talk with you
and you will know each other.
If you do not talk to them
you will not know them,
and what you do not know
you will fear.
What one fears
one destroys.

Chief Dan George

Wolf Now And Then

O'siyo my brother...now that we are face to face
we can see yesterday and tomorrow

In your eyes that... look of hunger
The look backward to yesterday
and the wonder,question of where have they gone
You do not remember the days.. of the new dawn

Aye.. for you have slept..
and the days passed into years
Yet are now felt of my todays tears

The heat of battles won and lost
Given over to the extreme cost
Here we stand...
looking into tomorrow..
and back to yesterday
Your eyes of yellow.. mine of green.
We both.. remembering the past and thinking
will we last this famine of the future and past.
Will tomorow return the days of yesterday

Somewhere inside we know the answer...

Spirit Warriors

I watched a swirling dervish of white
As it settled in for the night
Knowing all to well, what the wind would bring
As the night wore on ,I sat to listen
I heard your memories sing
Far off from heavens glisten
Howling in despair at the wind
The heartaches of times past
High above the moon shown brilliant
Throught the snowy mists
As the tree branches moaned in twists
Echoes of your shattered dreams
Scattering the pieces in icy streams
Chills of winters blast in spine tinglings
As regret mimicks forgotten minglings
Oh Spirit Warriors ...your haunting
spirit lingers, and my soul you caress,
with icy claws.
From the jagged peaks and hills you once roamed
Man must learn the lesson and pause..
Remembering that this to..was once your home
To hear the howling of the wind,
and heed the wisdom brought therein.

Warrior Story Of Yesteryear

Across the deep purple sky
The Guardian Warrior rides
Twin tomahawks at his side
He rides a white stallion with nostrils flaring red
Wild eyes glaring, leaving a trail of scattered stars
From jupiter to mars
Questing his goal.. his hearts desire
A raven haired beauty one who had stolen his soul
Reclamation upon his lips he swore damnation
His vengeance raged against the midnight sky
Clouds raced to clear a path
This warrior of old ,was filled with wrath
His prize of love to be found
Before the dawn upon earths ground
A vow he had made to keep her safe
To this he was bound
He had to leave her once
Now he returns to claim..
That which causes his heart to flame
His stallion lightly touching terra firma
Hooves of steel.made sparks of fire
Carries this warrior to reclaim his hearts desire
Upon the hill he spied her there,standing still
One swift sweep...
This night in his arms she would sleep
Many moons had passed

Since he had seen her last
Their love of old a memory
melted far in the past
Two souls would reunite
Upon this very night
Seems she had waited in sweet twilight
For this her warrior of old delight
Their love stolen once
By the white flame of long ago
Now fullfills a story of yesteryear

Trail Of Tears

Cherokee ,Chickasaw, Cree, Mohawk
Just a few that lost to the history of lies
Old Yellow Hair and his lips of double talk
Seminole, Lenapi Choctaw, Wyandotte
Great Nations under Fathers skies

He says lets take what they got
If they resist, each one dies
Land is what we need
Doesn't matter if (they bleed)
One by one or a thousand and one
This white man uses his gun
October 1838 skies... The march begins...
Let's see how many dies
For the land of these redskins

Little Star stood as if her feet were incased in concrete
The auctioneers gavel struck
Heart pounding and defiance upon her face
She felt the stab,as her heart shriveled and shook
As she heard the order to march!
No more would she see her family home place
Her throat constricted and parch
Sold to the highest bidder!

Days of hunger and cold so bitter
The Trail Of Tears
survived by only the fitter

Bloody road , unmarked graves,
Yet still echoes from yesterdays
Cherokee rose now grows
where fell to the ground their tears

As the Elders prayed for a sign
for mothers not to resign
Each tear drop became a rose
seven leaves on stem petal of white
and centers gold glows
On a clear night you can hear..
The echoes from the Trail Of Tears
A distant baby's cry upon the wind
Rain falling from a moonlit starry night
Moaning sorrow wafting across the land
Angel tears fell as they watched this sight
Perpetrated by lash and hand...
Four thousand Cherokee alone died

And the Spirits cried....

As the march labored on into November
The sleeting rain and snow claimed many more
That would not live to see December Some rode...

but most walked that bloody road
There's more to this story
yet to be told
You won't find it in your history book
The truth about all they took

Sit beside your grandmother and listen
Because she knows....
how the rest of this story goes.

Bonnie Ray

Loves Night Spirit

He sits alone beneath a raven moon
This aged warrior remembers his youth
For a few moments..he holds her once again
That love he shared that made his heart into truth
In the shadows she waits...as in years past ,long ago
He sees her face in the shadows of moon 's glow
His eyes close... and he feels her touch so soft

This woman sent to him..so very long ago
And once again they are in the barn's loft
The night is filled with the sounds of earth song all
around
Scents of sweet roses in her hair , fills his heart with
passion
And for hours the earth ceases to be beneath them.
Only the song of her soul is heard as they come down
together and touch the ground.
And in the stillness of night..he hears her call his name
from
afar.
He stands ...to follow her voice and whispers her name..
Then he realizes he was dreaming again.. and fate was
playing it's foolish game

Grandmother Was A Cherokee

Grandmother was a Cherokee
And folks loved her from all around
She had a gentle way about her
Her path was always heaven bound

In the night she was always there to comfort
With loving kindness and gentle care
Her ways much different than ours nowadays
But you can bet her love was always there

As I grew older and watched her age
She became more beautiful to me
Her face lined by life's history page
Eyes mirrored wisdom brightly

Among the greatest things she taught me...

Three things come to mind
Respect for the Elders and pride of family
To love Mother Earth and all mankind
And to walk my path honorably

She has gone to be with Great Spirit
But her loving touch is felt from time to time
Her stories and wisdom she left behind
I'm so proud Cherokee grandmother was mine

Cherokee Green Cherokee Blue

When in the deepest of the night
I feel so alone ..
The blood that runs in my veins
comforts me and calls me home
The drums of a far away time are my heart beat
Spirits of my Grandfathers call my name upon the night
winds
Grandaughter Grandaughter rejoice with your feet
Let your Spirit soar free upon Eagles wings
Come high upon the mountains and touch Father's sky
Grandaughter Grandaughter when you tire
Rest upon Mother Earth and listen to her sigh
Let your Spirit dance with the four winds
Like the smoke from ancient campfires
Grandaughter Grandaughter with eyes of green
Grandaughter Grandaughter hair of corn silk
Remember Remember and know you are seen
Stand up ,Stand up and be recognized
Grandaughter Grandaughter eyes of blue
Walk your path and remember where you been
Grandaughter Grandaughter,look within
Listen with your Spirit see with your heart
We Are One Spirit
Never are we apart
Authors note:
This poem is written and dedicated to all that have

Native American blood
They carry no card that identifies their heritage or tells
how much 'Indian 'they are.
Only the whispers of their heart to remind them.
For all that search and find and those that have been
erased by time

Run Free

If yesterday could be once more..
I'd run with the wind, in my hair
Ride my pony across the valley floor
Slay the dragon in his lair
Oh if yesterday could be once more
From the mountain peaks where Eagles soar
I'd spread my wings and fly ....
From the oceans deep I'd swim with dolphins
Oh if only yesterday... had stayed
There would be no need for cautions
I'd lay beneath the moon and count the stars
Once again I'd hunt the buffalo where they play
Paint my face with stripes and bars
Meet my love upon the path of yesterday
If only yesterday had not bid goodbye
and left me to ponder why..

Grandfather Calls My Name

From the mountains and the forests
I hear you Grandfather...
Your voice calls my name on the wind

From the valleys high and low
It matters not where I go
I hear you in the waters flow
I hear you in the falling snow
The winds that softly blow
High above.. you send Eagle Brother
To soar before my eyes
Calling me... you call from the skies

I am here Grandfather
With my heart I listen to your words
With my ears I hear...
Your message sent in song of birds
The warmth of my campfire tells me of other days
As flames rise in revealing rememberances
Talking in crackling voices, echoed old ways
In humble stillness..
Listening to yesterdays
I give you my willingness

Nights pass under the heavens,
in stories told of long ago

Bonnie Ray

I hear you Grandfather....
From the shadows of yesterday,
Tonight as I lay upon Mother Earths bed
I hear your gentle voice call
Upon the wind in the night
Your voice I hear in the rushing waterfall
Peace surrounds my campfires
I close my eyes and walk in dreams
Distant drums...beat ancient words
From high above in heavens streams

Upon A Painted Pony

Upon a painted pony two lovers did ride
One day soon she'd be his bride
Upon the path they'd walk as one.
In days to come she'd bear his son.
In days of yore these two were lore
In history's pages now live ever more
The legends told of Indian War

Their peaceful life was shattered
The children of earth were scattered
The long journey she did make
A trail of tears in her wake
Within her womb a son to come
His blood line lives on yet today
Related to you and me they say
In quiet moments alone..listen
With your heart you will know
A distant hoofbeat in the snow

Hear Me My Sister

My beautiful sister, please hear me
These words come from my heart ..to yours
A long time ago events beyond our control
separated us, you and I
When the white eyes came to our land
Our great great grandmother was taken away
she was made a slave to this foreign man
But in her veins the blood was pure Cherokee
And there is where I came from..to be me
The blood was passed to me from years passed
And thought my eyes are blue,
my heart and blood are Cherokee true
Though my skin be white, underneath it is red
My heart hears the drums
From the Ancient Ones
They have not forgotten me!
Time has tried to widen the trap
But together we shall close the gap
I hear grandfather speak in my ear
He tells me not to shed tears, but put away my fears
To never forget who I am!
And I ask you my sister..not to forget me
For I have not forgotten you
Awaken your heart..and remember
I reach my hand across the time span
to grasp my sisters hand

Bonnie Ray

I have traveled many roads
trying to find my way home
Come take my hand ..it will lighten both our loads

I Have No Indian Name

I Have No Indian Name
I am a Spirit without a name
Riding upon the winds of fame
My heart is free and glides through the sky
Upon the spirit of the winds on high
From the highest peak you will hear me call
In search of my name stolen at birth
Bt those that came to pillage Mother Earth
Throughout the ages the drums have beat
with the song of the chosen
I search the times and tides for my name
Lost in the times of greed and shame
Before my sun sets I shall reclaim
That which will identify my remains
The blood of warriors runs in my veins
And my heart is chosen true
Along the trail they died and bled
Trail of tears rain of the dead
Now the spirit in the wind
Shall whisper back to me
The wisdoms of my ancient grandfathers
To break the spine of greed and shame
My heart will then sing my name
Across the mountains and the plain
And destiny will beat the cheaters game

Bonnie Ray

Spirit In The Wind II

Never far apart ..you and I
As I sweep ...
from Mother Earth to Father Sky
For I am
The Spirit in the Wind
Ancient and wise
It is I..
That know your secrets from within
As you whisper them I grasp and
carry the to The Creator on high
For I am his messenger in disguise
Upon my breath Brother Eagle soars
Across this land from Mother Earth
To heavens shores
As autumn arrives ...hear my call
Watch as the leaves begin to fall
In spring my mighty breath
the leaves caress....
In summer...
Grandfather Sun will warm you
As I cool you with a welcome breeze
Before winters cold chill cause you to freeze
I Am
The Spirit In The Wind
Sometimes your foe , but more often your friend
I carry the sound of Brother Wolf..

As he howls in hunger or anguish at the moon
Sometimes I will awaken you from dreams
I carry many upon my wings
Listen as I join my Wolf brother
in his nightly sings
Often in the night listen
you can hear the distant Loon
upon the lake..
As he calls to his mate
From long ago.. .listen and know
The heart beat of ancient drums
as they tell the story of footprints in the snow
And the unkindness of long ago
Listen close my friend , you cannot catch
nor hold me in your grasp
I am free
For I am
Spirit In The Wind

December Snow Moon v s gi ga

December Snow Moon v s gi ga
As the winds of winter surround me
In this month of the snow moon
I look towards the heavens and see
The stars above that once were ours
Remembering the nights you and I
would lay in our lodge and make love for hours
Outside the wind would echo the lonliness of
the she wolf as she mourned her mate
Now it is I ....that am alone
and share her song of fate

The buffalo robe you gifted me
I wrap around me and feel your spirit near
As the month of the snow moon deepens
My heart yearns to hold you near
Far off upon the mountain
the cougar screams as her prey is taken
And the circle completes again
When my journey is at it's end my love
I will join you above
And once again we shall gather the stars
that once were ours

Sweet Twilight

Twilight cast a shadow deep
Where upon her pillow
She lay,in slumber deep
A dream of her Cherokee
In sunset meadows of wildflowers
Brings a memory
Of days gone and
old ways lost
Where once he came to lay beside her
Wrapping her in loves sweet embrace,placing
A kiss upon her tearstained face...
Now the Angel hovers near.. to take her
To her Cherokee dear.
Where once again..
They'll lay in sunset fields of wildflowers...
Tomorrows promise sweet and clear..

Bonnie Ray

Mother Earth Speaks

Mother Earth Speaks
Beneath the full winter moon of gold
I stood quietly and still...
and breathed in the scent of Mother Earths winter cold
High upon a branch , came the hoot of brother owl
Such wisdom he imparts to be one of fowl
Long into the night I listened to sounds of the night song
Far across a distant meadow came the cry of brother wolf
His mourning of mans stupidity cried all night long
A chill ran down my spine..
Omens being sung aloud as.. I stood beneath that old
pine
Ancients returned to places they had walked before
Ancestors perhaps yours and mine coming thru that
portal of time
They cry upon the wind and hide their eyes, on this scene
they abhor
Listen as the night speaks..
Winds blow through the night in mournful whine
Mother Earth speaks her heart in the night
if we but pause and listen....
Her story she will tell us true
Clouds pass high above hiding stars glisten
Long ago the waters of earth sang in tinkling blue
now their song sings a mounful death dirge
As the fish gasp for breath one last time

And curse the greed of human scourge
Mother Earth awaits the time of Rainbow Warrior
Soon they will come to undo the destroyer
The night begins to fade to silver and gray
As I stand in awe of her palette she puts on display
Mother Earth begins her song of a new day

Bonnie Ray

56

Talking Thunder

Beneath the darkened sky I watched with wonder.
As above me, I heard Talking Thunder.
At first he rumbled in a muffled grumble,
then Brother Wind brought the sound in a rolling rumble

A voice of authority, used to being heard far and wide
This giant of Talking Thunder
flying across the sky like a flock of ancient birds
Foretelling the future in Mother Natures words

Like an omen in the blackened sky,
Soon the pitter patter of rain drops
As if he had a reason to cry.

Flashing lightning cracked and stung the trees
with the fierceness of red flaming arrows.
A sight to bring even the bravest to their knees
I felt the earth shaking at the voice of Talking Thunder

As if Mother... were encouraging him to make her laugh.
Then suddenly.. the sky opened in a wide span ,
And gave Her, Our Mother a bath.

She danced in abandon as she shook the trees
in dancing, playful glee.

Bonnie Ray

While bolts of lightning flashed in answer to her plea.
She sang a song of thanks to Talking Thunder

Threads Of Life

From the day we are born
we spin the threads of life
Our own web so to speak
Threads that are both weak and strong
they weave our rights and wrong
The goals we set forth to seek
Our goodness and our bad that we wreak
We look back upon each strand with
either love, hate or happiness and yes even regret.
For the web of life spins either silver or gold
some with warmth, and some that leave us cold
We are afterall..... mere mortal human
Our hearts can touch with love or hate and spite
But when the web is finished we are left
with either a weak web or one of insight
We only know how good our web was
by the many or few that come to say goodbye
the word of kindness, and the eyes that cry
Or the grieving heart that looks toward heaven
And asks God why

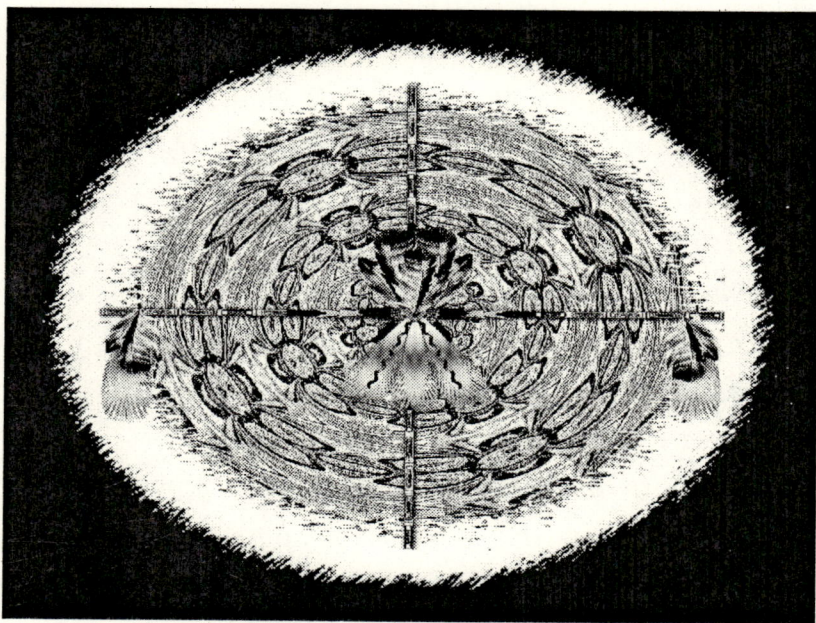

Awaken

The Drums have called my name
From my sleep of long ago
Listen too ! They may be calling you
Many years ago...
I walked upon this ground
With The People among them as one

Today I am returned to walk once again
I hear the crys of the ghostly wind
And yes my brother Wolf
Do you...
Listen to the song of the flute
It will lift your spirit to soar
With brother Eagle

Listen to Mother Earth she crys
The heart beats are out of time
She tells us...and asks us whys

Awaken

Bonnie Ray

Glorious Morning

My morning...
began with the song of the Robin
Telling me Spring is here
A look out my window,
I saw my friend, his message clear
Then came my friend Red Bird
Joining in with the chorus,
with his sweet melodic word
How glorious the morning song
Makes me know..
God is in His Heaven
And He will right the wrong
Spring is the renewal of all
a new beginning to embrace
and answer Mother Earths call
Time to plant the seeds of life
for God's creatures and flowers alike

Path Of Peace

Though I walk, live and drive upon
these streets of concrete
And hear the sounds of traffic and horn beep
I am who I am and always will be
Child of Creator and of Cherokee

Once long ago I ran free as the wind
It did not matter I had no money to spend
My life was rich and blessed
by Great Spirits Hand.
We were as children and lived off
this beautiful land.

Elders taught us the meaning of life
by wisdoms learned told around the campfires
For centuries my people have been Earthkeepers
Whatever we take from Mother Earth we put back

Today the Spirits of my grandfathers ..
call to me to remember to love Mother Earth
as she loves us. To give love and comfort
to those in need. To bind the hearts
torn by strife and greed

To love our brothers and sisters
and to raise our children with pride and honor

Bonnie Ray

For if we respect and love each other
and this great land
And allow our hearts to be touched
by Great Spirits Hand

What is there to fight over?

Singing River

As I sat beside the river I heard her heart singing
She told me stories of long ago
Of the folks that crossed her wide span with hopes and
dreams
Tales of good crossings and some that were so sad
Wagon wheels that got lost in the mud
Battles that once raged with hatred
and her beauty was streaked with blood
She sang to me of once peaceful villages that dwelt upon
her banks
Her song sang soft .....
her song sang of the Eagles that soared aloft
The melody sometimes sweet and serene
Other times it would almost scream
This river sang her song to me
Her mirrored surface reflected sky of blue
Clouds of white...
She sang of the little boy that yelled in delight
as he caught his first fish
Saddness changed the melody as she told of the baby
that was lost and she washed it upon the shore to his
mother safely
She sang of two lovers that shared their first kiss upon
her shore
Then twenty five years later they returned once more
And I sat there listening long past the fading light
As this river sang me her song that made me smile,
made me cry .... long into the night

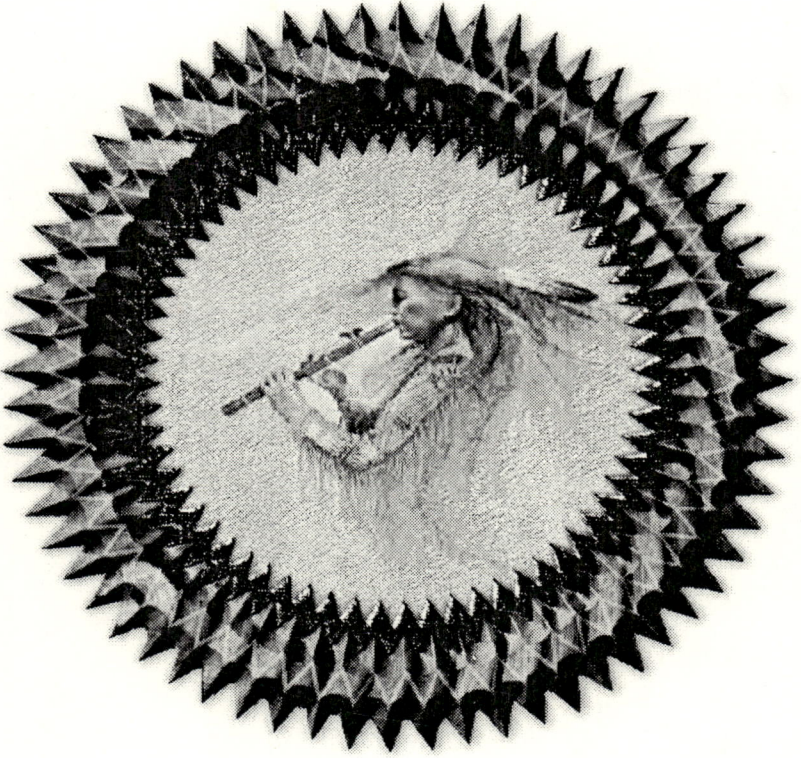

Uncle Raliegh

In the evening light I still hear his flute
His songs he played for me as a child
Uncle Raliegh , my mentor and kin to boot
He always believed in me and never thought of me as
wild
The scent of pine and coal soot, still bring me a smile
Hard working man of the railroad ,traveled many a mile
Uncle Raliegh never let me forget my Cherokee root
I can still hear his voice saying "never forget"
Sometimes in the night I hear that lonesome train whistle
And I remember back through childhood,wildflowers and
thistle
To a wickiup of mud and sticks and happy hours
Where Uncle Raliegh told me stories of that family of
ours
He taught me how to listen to the bird song and hear the
singing of the brook.
He taught me to see with my heart and to hear to the
stories in the wind
These he taught me without even opening a book
What priceless gifts he gave to me way back then
And when his sun set,and he went home..
With him .a part of me he took
Dedicated to CherokeeRose
thank you for sharing Uncle Raliegh

Bonnie Ray

From The Mountain Far

From The Mountain He Came
He said ..I have come from the far mountain
To show you the way home
You have one more task to do before we go
Grandfather has sent me, so you won't travel alone
The road ahead is long and you will tire
I'll be here to lift you up and share the load
So you may walk with ancestors and honor
upon the good red road

Chapter Two
Inspirational Poems

This chapter is for inspiration and spiritual hope
We all have those days when we ask why me Lord?
In here are some poems, I hope bring you peace and comfort.

Morning Praise

From greening branches of new spring
an early morning song did ring
High upon the mornings breath
A praise of thankfulness did sing

Mighty in his belief of life
Though it be fraught with strife
Hard the winters cold chills
He with his faith has survived
Gives forth his sweet trills

Greatful for every crumb and seed
Proof that the Lord does provide
His every need

A lesson for man yet to learn
This simple truth yet to discern
His Eye is on the sparrow
And yet man chooses to sorrow
In his quest to borrow
Will overlook the treasures
Awaiting him tomorrow

Bonnie Ray

A Perfect Rose

As I stood at the rivers edge
There before me a mirrored image of a rose
Shining through the glass surface, in mirrored wedge
One perfect red rose
Where it did come from..
only Heaven knows
Perhaps an Angel planted it there
Just to show me that
God does care
For as I reached to touch the rose
I heard a voice say....
Only God in Heaven makes
The perfect rose..yourself
He makes no mistakes
His love in many ways, invisibly shows
For more oft than not..as mortals be
Only God in Heaven knows
We at times are to blind to see
Where the river of our life flows

Autumn And Sunsets

As the evening sun sets upon the earth
So does it set upon each life
In time......
we shed our earthly cares and strife
The colors of our own sunset
reflect back to how we once lived
We leave behind remnants for those we hope
remember us with love and kindness
Praying we shone a light in the darkness
that took away the blindness
Much like the sun as it melts into the sea
at dusk there are a few streaks left lingering
across the sky ... a fading memory
To those that knew and loved you and I
Some were there to witness our birthing sunrise
others only share in the glory of our day
While some walk with us every step of the way
stopping only long enough ....in our waning
to kneel and pray
Our lives may have been tempestuous like the sea
or quiet as the falling leaves of autumn.
Life the gift...drifts away before we know it
Just like the sunsets that leave behind their beautiful
memory.
So do we....
Like Autumn and Sunsets

His unfailing love guideth you and me
A Humbling Rose

As twilight began to cast
I saw the shadow upon the rose
It seemed so sad ,dusk had past
And another day came to a close
I touched the velvet petals so soft
And felt the pain it had bourn
To become the beauty that it was
The struggle it survived to be born
I thought once, to pluck, and shelter in a vase
Just then my hand it pricked, by thorn
Reminding me , it was not my choice, or place
To decide it's final fate
Best left to the Master Gardener
I walked away in humbled state...
Leaving it where it grows
A lesson taught by..
the humbling rose

The Floor Of Heaven II

As I watched her sweep the sky
Her magical broom swept
both... low and high

Spanning the western sky
I watched in awe and wept
The blues , pinks and golds
This wondrous scene unfolds

As our Creators housekeeper
goes about her evening chores
As she turned down the lights
on just one more blending
of God's grandeur

I marveled again..
as she took my breath away
While she swept the floor of heaven
Blushing reds and pinks, deep
shades of blues,
as the sun sank deep....
in multitude of hues

I could only watch and weep
At the beauty glittered gold
Pastels of the Masters easel

Bonnie Ray

While the sun melted deep

She began turning on
Heavens nightlights..
Venus , Mars and Aries
Jupiter and Saturn,the Milky way
All these took my breath away

As the sun closed his eyes
One last sweep....
across heavens skies

Sweet Mother Earth..
had closed the shades
As yet another
glorious day fades

October's Reflection

Octobers reflection upon the stream
A mural of natures aged beauty
An artists ideal scene
Mother nature fullfills her duty
As dusk begins to enter night
A reflection of the fading day
Mirrors colored treasures delight
Evening song begins a serenade
in testament of life
And what God has made
As I walk beside still waters basking
in the beauty of October's reflection,
The water makes a ripple,as a bass glides by
in evenings meditation
Frogs begin their evening symphony
as if a command performance they present to me
And I am reminded, by October's reflection
That God is everywhere...

Nature's Grace

As the dove sings her morning song
Honeyed dew drips from the rose
Sunrise serenade has began ablaze
Gently as the willow branch blows
In sweet warmth of summers daze
Fresh scent of jasmine fills the air
As morning breaks in beauty
Roses open in rainbows fair
In the meadow wildflowers gloss
From the winds mellow toss
In moments of soft embrace
Morning begins with the innocence
of nature's grace

Bonnie Ray

Multicolored Friends

Welcome friends as..
Into my yard you gather
Feeder is filled with seed
Some sunflower and thistle
A great feast upon which to feed
You bless me with your song or whistle
Why some even sound like a reed
Cheerfully you...share with me
Oh how......I appreciate thee
I filled the bird bath...with fresh water
To keep you clean as you wish
The pond does flow to wash down the fodder
There is old Blue Jay he will holler and screech
As upon the wire he sits......to preach
Not a seed will he..with you...share
Pay him no mind...we have plenty to spare
And there is the White Dove
Come to coo....and tell me of her love
Time goes too quickly......I whisper
But they tomorrow will return by and by
As on the wing again..........they fly

His Quiet Impression

Beneath the black velvet sky... stars glisten
Looking down upon earth, they give off their quiet
impressions.
God is watching over all... and is waiting there to listen.
Their quiet shining... is His gentle way of reminding
Look up....Such magnificience in His designing
His soft touch upon our heart, leaves a quiet impression
Forgiving us our daily transgression
With Loves everlasting prints of quiet forgiveness
Faith is renewed by His quiet impressions
That certain feeling we get when we know we are not
alone
An Angel beside us guiding us home
That invisible unseen hand holding us safely
Leaves us feeling blessed. for truly..
It does leave an everlasting quiet impression

Bonnie Ray

Morning Glories Twine

As the day breaks and begins anew
Morning Glories...
From my window ....shades of white, pink and blue
simple little flowers twine round the old pump
Not flashy or hybrid , not even particular
They'll even grow round an old stump
Beautiful in their simple way
This unpretentious little flower
Blooms everyday...sweet even in repose
Like the Trumpet flower it vines
And in the late evening it will close
It gives a message .....if we but read it
That life is a journey of many paths
We twine the path, much like a vine
A twist, a turn, a curve or straight line
And with a little love ,a smile ,a caring touch
We too blossom ....in the sunshine
Each in our own given hue
Everyday we arise to our own
Morning Glories Twine

Pieces Of The Heart

For everyone that enters our heart through loves door
When they leave they carry a part of you
Forevermore

Some take more than others
While those we loved the most..
take only , as much as we allow
Then some come back again
only to take a second bow

We give our love so freely
when we are young
And as we grow older and wiser
we learn to listen...
to the song thats being sung

We have no guarantee ...
how long we will still love the melody
But for everyone that enters through our hearts door
They carry away a part of you and me.
Forevermore

Bonnie Ray

Rainbows And Storms

Fresh and sweet the air from the cool rain
Like a balm to Mother Earth washing away her pain
Hail beating the rythmn of the storm upon the tarmack
As if it were the percussion section drumming in the back

Overhead the sky is hidden from sight by the fog
Flora and fauna alike embrace the rain
As they dance in the breeze of rains sog

Quiet hush falls all around
As if the rain takes a breather
Even crickets cease their singing sound

While overhead the thunder grumbles and talks
Then just as suddenly as it came to being ......it stops

Water pools in the streets
Flooding the sidewalks
As rain, sweet rain , has given life back, in refreshing
sheets.

Overhead the sky has cleared and there is Gods rainbow
All seven glorious colors, a spectrum of pure delight
Blue skies and sunshine once again
Gods beautiful sight,

He sent to you and I my friend
Rainbows and Storms

Bonnie Ray

Touch His Morning

In the quiet before dawn
touch the softness in the air
You will find, His Presence that's
patiently waiting there
A precious moment with Him
Our glorious Lord and Friend
When the sun begins to peek above the horizon
God is smiling upon His canvas
The mist that suspends just o'er the mountains
are His tears of happiness
That kisses the earth in sweet bless
An arch becomes a rainbow
He is the calming peace
that will forever bestow

Yes Lord

In the quiet of first morn's light
I heard my Lord say.
It will be alright
Even though your heart be troubled
I will guide you through
But I said...
Lord?
How can that be true
When the world has stopped believing in you
They say you are dead!
And this is what my Lord said
Does not the sun rise?
And I said yes Lord
Does the rainbow appear after rainy skies
And I answered...yes Lord
Do you still see the stars I hung in heaven?
I answered yes Lord
Do the church bells ring on day seven?
Of course, I answered yes Lord
Do the birds still sing?
Yes Lord they sure do
Do the flowers bloom in spring
Yes Lord ,I sneeze every year
Do the seasons change?
Well yes... Lord they surely do
Then He said...good glad to hear that

Well I've got to go, but I'll be close by
I've got a million things yet to do
I'll be seeing you in the by and by
Ohh by the way, tell them I still live!
This world does not run on automatic pilot

When I was Five

I remember the picture
it hung upon our family home wall
As a child I used to be afraid of it
It was Grandmothers favorite one of all
The eyes would follow me around the room
I felt the Presence of the Saviour
As passed Him.... I would zoom
Looking up at Him ... from far below
At the age of 5 running as fast as I could go
Grandmother would tell me never fear
The Lord.... is watching over you dear
My family always revered the Word
She would hush my fears , and dry my tears
While I feeling kind of foolish and absurd
She would tell me of Jesus and the things He did
Of the time of flood and the olive branch
and the snow white bird.
Of how He would tell the children
of their Father on high
The One that lived way up in the sky
How one day we all would meet
In the sweet by and by

Now that I am old and looking toward my sunset
I look over at that picture of Him
and know He still.... watches over me yet.

Bonnie Ray

And in His Eyes
I am the innocent of long ago
Back when I was five years old

Puzzle Pieces

High above in a sky of pale blue,
I watch big white clouds drift,
In puffy sets of three and two.
Looking like puzzle pieces strewn..
by the carelessness.. of an invisible giant foot
As they drift... in search of the perfect fit,
to a masterpiece painting.
Below them a pattern of green leafy lace stirs from a
gentle breeze.
While flashes of redbirds , bluejays , blackbirds,and
sparrows,
fly swiftly from limb to limb, straight as arrows.
All unmindful the part they play,
in this beautiful tapestry of life
That sassy bluejay scolds, the wren once again.
As she beats him to the birdfeeder... in secret revenge.
The soft distant cooing of the rain crow ...
Calling for rain and the beautiful rainbow.
Upon the birdbath the robin takes a sip.
Whilst high upon a limb, a redwing waits his turn to
take a dip.
Puzzle pieces all unaware...
they have finished the puzzle
Unaware they are... natures Puzzle Pieces

Chapter Three
Love Poems

When The Music Stops

When the music stops and this ole heart stops speaking
Will you come look for me in the words... seeking
Should the sky be gray ,will you come to read
my heart , to find a sunny day.
Sweetheart the words are true,
Just remember I wrote them for you.
On a midnight in the quiet of night
Will you come to read the light.
On an early Sunday morn
will you remember when our love was born
When you hear the Whip O Wills song
Will you... for me long
Sweetheart the words are true,
Just remember...
I wrote them for you
When the music stops

Bonnie Ray

Maybe Someday

If I could write my heart on paper
It would tell you how much you mean to me
I never been one to say much
Afraid and shy and scared of goodbyes
Because my heart.. has been broken by life's touch
But when I see you appear...
I think how much you mean to me dear
You are my inspiration and my sunshine
Someday .....O how I wish you would be mine
But afraid and shy and scared of goodbyes
I'll continue to love you from afar
But every night I'll look toward heaven
And ask God to protect you beneath an Angel's star
My heart will love you forever
Whether near or far
Please my love ..forget this never.
Maybe someday ...

My Special One

Gently as the waters flow
My love for you does grow
Soft and pure as new snow

Sometimes my love swells over the banks
When times I look in your eyes and see your returned love
I look towards heaven and silently give thanks
For I truly know you are a gift from up above

My Special One... today I send you my heart
It sings your name inside my breast
Hold it close my love, never our love to part

Forever yours until it goes to rest
Like the rivers forever flowing
Our love withstands times test

Bonnie Ray

Something Somewhere Sometime

Something in you...saw Something in me
And Something in me ...recognized
Something in you...

Did we meet Somewhere ...in a faraway world...
Was there a time you loved me and I loved you to
Sometime.... once long ago

Has the past met up with the present
My dear ..I sure hope so

Life gives us pebbles to polish effervescent
You are the jewel I have found
in the stream of my life

Yes Somewhere , Sometimes , Somethings

I would have known you Anywhere,
Anytime , Anyplace
Because Some things are bound forever
Like you and I

Until

Until time is only a faded memory
Your touch is branded for all eternity
Until the earth is only a dying ember
My love...you...I will remember
Should the clock still my heart
I'll carry your love to where ever..
my heart does surrender
Your love and I... shall never part
When the sands of time steal away
To some far distant day
I'll still be yours, and wait for you
Upon those far distant shores
To once again whisper your name
Rekindling our loves burning flame
For ,time cannot erase or misplace
My loves beautiful face
For love is never mere fantasy
it is the only , constant reality

Time In A Drawer

As she opens the drawer
Of the old chest
Finding treasures
She loved best
Memories flood her mind
As they walk back thru time
An old photograph of herself
When younger,
That use to sit upon a loved ones shelf
A ribbon from a special bouquet
Given from a lover
On her sixteenth birthday
A tiny childs footprint
On a piece of paper
She saw,
A reminder of her motherhood
And the one who calls her Ma
The years flew by so swift
As thru time in a drawer
She did sift
Glancing at the cloock
On the wall 3:00A.M.
Her mind races on
Remembering times bygone
Heartaches and memories
Of laughter and tears

Sifted thru time in a drawer
Walking thru the years
Slowly she picks up the mirror
As she glances at her reflection
She realizes that time is a gift
Given to us by Gods timely perfection

Bonnie Ray

Play For Me Maestro

Like an arpeggio
played by a maestro upon the piano
You touch my heart with your loves melody
I carry it with me wherever I go

You put a smile on my lips knowing,
it was composed just for me
The passion of your heart I hear in every note
Sweet and more romantic than any rhapsody
Anyone ever wrote

So my love, I send you the key of C
to begin again your melody for me
It unlocks the door to my heart
Enter in and never depart

Gossamer Whisper

Upon a gossamer whisper
I heard you call my name
And rushed to awaken
As in dreams I slept
To discover that in my
Heart you will be kept
This restless heart
Shall never be the same
Because a gossamer whisper
Has called my name

Bonnie Ray

It Is Because

When you find a card in your mail from me
It is because I love you
When I reach across the miles and touch you
It is because I love you
When your day is dark and I drop in to say hi
It is because I knew and I love you
When your smile is upside down and I turn it around
It is because I love you
When I share your laughter and tears
it is because I love you
When I say a little prayer for you
It is because...
I love you

Will You Love Me Tomorrow

Will you love me tomorrow
As much as today
even when I'm old and grey.
Will you love me tomorrow
as much as today.... even
When age is showing
will you still hold my hand
and tell me you are my man
When the road ahead leads us
to golden years
Will your heart and lips
say......... I love you dear
I'm right beside you have no fears
And should I go first
will you let me go with a kiss
while holding me close
and say ..you my love I will miss
If your answer is yes
then I know
God did me Bless
And I shall wait for you
at Heavens Door
Till you can hold me again
once more..

Bonnie Ray

Credit Card

Credit card issued to you my love
From the one who love you
Interest free no annual fee
Please use it lovingly
Meant for card holder only
Will never leave you lonely
Please keep it close at hand
Your wish is it's command
Limit amount? Unlimited for user
This card carries a no limit clause
From the Bank Of Just Because
If for some reason it is lost or stolen
Please report to me
For you see it is golden
Created for young and olden
Discover it's possibilites
You won't be dissappointed
It is issued from my heart
By the Bank Of Just Because
And me..the one who loves you

Stairway To My Heart

If I could build a starirway to my dream
to share my heart and love with you
It would begin at the garden gate
A garden where roses bloom from care and love
Watered by sweet Angels tears from above
A path leading to a 'home' built with my heart
and you in mind,
From which you would never wish to depart
From the window glows the candles light
showing you the way in the darkest of night
The footpath would be lighted by glowing stars
Music from the harps and violins of maestros
would play serenades as you began the first step
to enter upon the stairway to my heart...
Your journey to me would be filled with wondrous
sights of a magical paradise only dreamed by you and I
Where the hour glass of time never runs out
and our hearts never experience hurt or doubt
With each step you take love strengthens and grows
And each new day ends in glorious sunset flambeaus
as we sit in the garden of roses watered by Angel tears
As our love blooms and lives throughout eternitys years
Enjoying the colors of life's rainbows

Bonnie Ray

Written For You

As each year passes I think back and treasure
each moment we shared
The days we laughed and together cried
Times we told each other we really cared
Shared hopes and dreams that have lived and died
And though you have never held me in your arms
I know in my heart....
Side by side ,we'll help each other weather life's storms
But as ever I will bide
Miles separate us now
But I know it won't always be that way..somehow
For it was written upon the wind
You were made for me...and
I was made for you my love and my friend
Our paths have taken different turns
But we will meet one day
Because like a circle...love returns

True love always finds it's way

Dreams

In the stillness of night I sit alone
thinking of you..
It is the middle of the night and I picture you
Snuggled warm in your bed
I want to hold you in my arms
And whisper to you , things I've never said
Ever so softly , not to awaken you
Like a sweet dream you once knew
And when the dawn breaks and you awake
you'll remember me as a sweet dream
One that you'll try to dream again
searching for that lovers scene
Recapturing the softness of the love you felt
surrounding you ...in your dream
In dreams where we laughed and played
and love will never fade
And as dawn breaks I leave you
softly with a kiss
In the arms of Morpheus

Bonnie Ray

What Price Love

What price love
Can you buy it?
~~~~<<>>~~~~
No for it will be imitation
Did it fall from above?
Or is it just your imagination
~~~~<<>>~~~~
Only for a few moments will it have a star studded cast
Like a new pair of shoes
The shine will fade too fast
~~~~<<>>~~~~
When the new wears off your boughten love
Love leaves a memory to haunt from the past
~~~~<<>>~~~~
Love comes in many facets,
like a diamond cut by a master
~~~~<<>>~~~~
You'll only see the sparkle, as he fashioned it
~~~~<<>>~~~~
Love that strange emotion!
We all chase it , need it, crave it
Spins our world in red or blue revolution
~~~~<<>>~~~~
Love can be deep or shallow
Depending on the seeds depth
Plant love fertile, not fallow

~~~~<<<>>>~~~~

Love a beautiful gift, a beautiful emotion
Give It.. you won't regret it

Bonnie Ray

Teddy Bear Love

In my arms he snuggled each night
My teddy bear friend ,that I loved
He was so soft and always felt so right
I knew he would never leave me blue
Funny I remember him after all these years
But he reminds me ..of you
You're always there to wipe away my tears
There you are..arms opened wide
waiting to turn my world around
Ohh how I loved my teddy bear friend
He meant the world to me, way back then
I so glad that I have you
Because you're my real teddy bear
I'll never outgrow loving you

Just A Four Letter Word

Just a 4 letter word
The kindest you ever heard
Love
Loves lips kiss one softly
Loves arms hold one tenderly
Over the world and all around town
Love is given ever so sweetly
Makes one act like a clown
Venus goddess of love
has given one a little shove
Cupid with his bow
touches the heart with a glow
Everyone is susceptible
Just a 4 letter word
To all it is acceptable
Love
Spins the world around
Turns one inside out and upside down
Love
Is it only a 4 letter word ?
Such a small word with such a big meaning
L is for a lifetime to love
O is over all things it will overcome
V is for volume of trust
E Is for every heart and soul in need

Bonnie Ray

Just a 4 letter word
In thought and deed

Loves Grace

So tender your love ...
that wraps me in it's embrace
My love ..I'm so greatful to have found your loving grace
Thoughts of you bring a smile to me even in my darkest
hours
For I know, no matter what, your love is given with
grace

Like the sunshine kissing upon the rose bowers
When we are parted and life feels empty and cold
It is in your heart ...where I find your warmth and my
place
As time rushes away so quickly,
I pray to be in your arms- as we grow old

Each night I pray to the Goddess of Love, for enough
time
Our love...more precious than diamonds and gold
Passion will stand beside us....forever

Always... I'll be yours and you'll be mine
And the Angels will guide our steps ...
until the twelvefth of never

So tender your love, so lucky am I

Bonnie Ray

Hold tight the dreams within
Love with grace never bids goodbye

Autumns Blaze

In autumns love of fire
You are still my hearts desire
As I watch the glow from
Autumns beautiful show
Your memory haunts me anew
In colors of rust and gold
I remember your kisses
Sweet as morning dew
Love in your eyes aglow
Told me everything
I wanted to know
Your heart was mine
As I became thine
A love meant to be
Still and always
Waits for thee
In autumns glow
Or winters snow
My love..belongs to you
And will always show
You will feel me close
In autumn,springtime,
summer,
Or winters sleepy repose
You are the one I chose.

Bonnie Ray

Loving Me

Time cannot erode ....
the love you have give me bestowed
For time though it be eternal..so is your love
You my dear are always there
with comfort and care
Each new dawn as I arise
I am assured that it is you
that makes my happiness
and blue skies
A kind word , a soft hello
a sweet smile come to me
Fresh as a morning flowered meadow
your love daily blooms
I'm so glad there's you
My heart and soul loves you true

Tears Of Time

Time is my worst enemy, because I can't change the clock
If only I could just sit down with you and talk
I gave you my heart...... from the very first hello
Everytime I saw you..My heart skipped a beat
And....my knees turned to jello

Maybe back then I should have told you so
But afraid and shy....I let every chance pass me by
Your words always touched my heart
Some even made me cry ....

I prayed to God above to never let us part
Somehow God wasn't listening in
but he did make you my friend

Tears..... I've shed a million down thru time....
because you would never be mine.
Not a day goes by that I don't think of you
And on the days, I don't see you..I worry to
Those are the days I'm so blue

Until the clock stops ticking
I'll continue to love you ...
If for no other reason than..
just because you are you

Bonnie Ray

Through time and eternity
And beyond infinity......
But darling, from a distance...
for my heart can't stand the pain

I would need to hold you close
if you were near
so I'll just stand apart
and hold you in my heart dear

And... shed.
These tears of time

Blindly My Heart

Like a shadow in the silence of night
And blindly as a child of the light
My heart reaches out to you with all it has to give
I see you in glowing perfection
Each day you are my reason to live
Without a flaw of any detection
You are my only hearts direction
Tender are my thoughts moments
From morning to night
Precious as a rare jewel
Your embrace of heavens delight
Each day my feeling grows blindly
No thought of the morrow
Please my dear accept it kindly
Fear not I , bring you no sorrow
Silent as a shadow in the dark of night
And blindly as a child of the light
You are my sweetest dream fullfilled
My heart feels you with every beat
Forever and 6 months past eternity
I greatfully lay my hearts feelings at your feet

Bonnie Ray

My Roses Of December

My roses of December are tucked away
Held within my heart, for a rainy day
Multicolored roses ,
Of joy ,tears ,love and laughter
Roses of many colors
That bloom for me here and everafter
Some I give to those I love
Others I only share with God above
If you should have a rose to spare
Give it to someone ..
that you know will care.
It will enhance their garden of
December Roses

God has given us our memories
so that we may have roses
in December

Run Don't Walk

Run don't walk to the nearest phone
I'll be waiting here at home
Say the words that are in your heart
Tell me you love me..we'll never part

Make our dream into reality
Open your heart and let me see
Cross the bridge into my arms
Let's set off fire alarms

Run.... don't walk

Pick up the phone and dial my number
and let's talk....talk talk

Play me a love song on your guitar
Let's make wishes upon our lucky star

Darling, please don't hesitate
Open your hearts gate

Hurry my love
You are my sunrise
You are my sunshine
I'm sure this is no surprise

Let's talk talk talk
Run ....don't walk

Bonnie Ray

Wonderful You

Wonderful you're always on my mind
My friend I love you
You always have a word so kind
The day we met ...was my lucky find
Always you seem to know when I'm blue
Asking is there anything you can do
My sweet friend .....
a treasured heaven send
What would I ever do without you
So I thought I should just tell you true
I thank you for turning my gray to blue
There is none ..so dear as you

Silence Of Gold

In the silence that deepens as night
Your love rings loud and clear
I hear it not with my ear
But my heart hears every word
My heart beats your name
Much like gentle sound of winged bird
or the rythmn of sweet summer rain
Miles separate us, but not the heart
For from there my love
you'll never part
Your memory rests in my heart
soft as an Angels breath
And as sweetly as the morning bird song
on a beautiful fresh spring day
Sometimes silence speaks louder
than any word you might say
As quiet moments shared unfold
In silence of gold

Bonnie Ray

Just For Today

Just for today I will love you
With all that I am
And all that I hope to be
God only gave me today
To do with as I may
Tomorrow is only a hope
But today I promise to love you
in every way
Should God give me tomorrow
I will love you that day to
But if I should not be here
Do not waste your day in sorrow
Just remember..I loved only you

Love Has Enemies

From the heart love is given
by young and old
Love struggles to survive the rigors of everyday livin'
This beautiful emotion with so many stories untold
Caught unaware when laid bare...
LOVE
innocent without so much as a care
Never thinking it needs to be aware
Love has enemies everywhere
From the four winds they blow
Here are just a few I know
Jealousy, Hurt, Anger, Fears
These bring the Distrust,and Tears
Misunderstanding sweeps in the door
and can hang around for evermore
Deceit of course will spread it's Lies
riding on lips of ancient history
that refused to accept goodbyes...
Yes love has enemies everywhere
So lover beware
Love Has Enemies

Bonnie Ray

Who Will Hold Me Then

When in my times of darkness and fear
I wonder.... who will be here..
today or tomorrow
To hold me , love me ,and chase away my fear
When loniliness surrounds me in sorrow
Will it be you?
That shines bright light of the morrow
When night winds call my name
and coldness clutches my heart
Will it be you? Or..
Will we still be.... so far apart
Who will hold me then?
Will it be you ?
That takes away my dark skies
Will it be you?
That kisses away the tears from my eyes
When time wears away my soul
and there are no more rainbows left in lifes
memory bowl
Will it be you ?
When my heart bleeds from loves thorns
Will you stop the flow
Or lay my body beneath the snow
Will it be you?
Who will hold me then

Softly Love

Love...yours
Soft and warm as a feather bed
wraps me from toe to head

Lips ...yours
Sweet and tender upon mine
like a fragrant heady wine

Eyes ...yours
Shine with loves fire
tell me I am your hearts desire

Arms ..yours
that hold me in loves sweet embrace
Vanquish my fears without a trace

Hands ..yours
Touch my being with tenderness
filling my heart with loves blissfulness

Heart...yours
Captured mine
Forever entwined

Souls.....ours
Meld together by loves powers
Softly Love

Bonnie Ray

Yesterdays Words

It keeps right on a hurtin...
those yesterdays words..once you spoke so certain.
Now the words remain behind.. that old final curtain
dropped on yesterdays stage...
fading to black from yesterdays page.
An old flame that haunts the new day we made
just for you and I
Oh will yesterdays words ever be forgotten?
Or will the pages refresh and the words somehow become
renewed?
Will in the dead of night ..your heart remember?
A line or two from yesterdays pages?
Will this love of ours be from....May to December
Darling... should that day come back...
And you find in your heart ..there is something you lack..
Tell me dear..and I will go...but..in my heart
I will forever know..once upon a page you wrote of love
just for me..I'll take the page and refresh it to read over
again
As I bring down the memories from yesterdays words
and recall ...somewhere in the dead of night,
I was just another page from your life.
But remember..I'll always love you.
Yesterday , today ,tomorrow and forever
as I write them in....tomorrows pages
While hiding the hurt ever so clever

Yesterdays Tomorrows

Yesterday echoes from distant places
Where once love and laughter thrived
Old memories of good times and bad
Haunt the halls of hearts that have cried
Dreams and promises reverberate in tones sad
Yet some live on by mere will power while others died
Yesterday gone cold as ashes from fires past
As memories drift away like dust in the wind
From dreams and promises never meant to last
Upon the new tomorrow we hang our new days dreams
And cast our fate to heavens shore
In hopes of better tomorrows that will never part at the
seams
As we pray pain and sorrow comes no more
In lifes foolish schemes.

Bonnie Ray

Every Now And Then

Every now and then..
I think of way back when,
The time of apple blossoms
with petals soft and sweet
Petals fell like white drifting snow
You held me close, whispered
how you loved me so.
Every now and then
I wish that I could go....
to way back then when.
Love was so simple way back then
Apple blossoms fell like white snow
as we walked beneath the moon glow
holding hands...every now and then
A sweet scent of apple blossoms
drifts past my window.
Someday again ..
perhaps I'll remember you...
every now and then

Sorrows Weeping Place

Where sorrow shows in every heart.
a man comes to know.
A place inside thats deep
and tries to sleep.
No pleasure does he find
when love is blind.
Once he loved a woman
then found her to be untrue
now he sits alone and blue
Someday ...he prays
his pain will go away.
The only promise he is given
is to meet on a distant golden shore
When life and love is so mistrusting
and treacherous.
He cannot let go and live dangerous.
For when the pain tries to sleep
in constant sorrow it keeps.
In the wind he hears his name
calling him to play the game
And then he knows ..
she was not the only one to blame
When a heart cannot speak
it is left in sorrow deep.
Lying there alone.. unable to sleep
for her love he could not keep
Now in sorrows weeping place...
they both are left to weep

Bonnie Ray

Loving Lies And Alibies

Ahhhh....tell me those sweet lies again
Can't get enough of them
Lie to me.... Lie to me,
Alibi to me, I can be..
whoever you want me to be.

Let me hear those love lies again
Honey don't you see..
Time will let you back in
I need those sweet lies ,
even those lying alibies
To get me thru the day
When you are not here, I hold them near

Those lies and loving alibies
I love to hear whispered... by you dear
So honey lie to me as long as you please
It will keep my heart at ease

Keep lying.... So I won't be dying
No tears left to be drying..
Only echoing footsteps to trace
Until I find that you ..
I can one day.... replace

Ahhh... lie to me... lie to me
Those sweet loving lies of yours
Are going to one day..open my eyes
to your lying hearts doors.
Keep lying.... So I won't be dying
No tears left to be drying..

Only echoing footsteps to retrace
Until I find... that you ..
I can one day.... replace.
Those lies and loving alibies
I love to hear whispered... by you dear
So honey lie to me as long as you please
It will keep my heart at ease

Bonnie Ray

By The Garden Gate

Love me not I prefer,
If loving me recalls her
Rather love me because I am me
And I am all you want to see

Don't try to clone or mold me
For I am truly one of a kind
As you let me wander through your mind
Remember me by the ties that bind

The love we shared and the time we spent there
Just remember to love me for me
You hold in your hand the key
That unlocks the door of loves memory

Because in your heart you really care
And when your new love breaks your heart
Tears you apart...

Remember me...I 'll be waiting
By the same Garden Gate
Where we said goodbye
on our last date

Undeleteably Yours

You can't delete my heart
only my email
You can't erase the memories
they return without fail

You can't burn loves bridge
it's made of loves steel
My love is forever undeleteable
this heart of love will always feel

Miles are as nothing between us
my heart is linked to yours
No X in the corner
that closes hearts doors

Love should never be played as game
For one will be left in pain
Another will maybe feel shame
Pride will call out...who's next?

And a broken heart dies vexed
I have left my loves prints
within your hearts doors
Which means...I am
Undeleteably yours

Shared Tears

I give to you my heart and soul.
I know without that..
No love.. will ever be whole.
Come to my world..
And stand by my side.
If my heart can comfort you.
You won't be denied.
I want to feel every teardrop.
When in darkness you cried.
I strove to remind you that those tears
Are also mine tonite .
Open your heart .
Open every secret door.
A shared life
Love..will remain... forever more.

Ages Of Love

I had a friend tell about their aged mother
She liked to read romance books
From cover to cover
So I thought about that
And this is what I discover
We may grow old and wrinkled
Eyes with laugh lines crinkled
But our hearts stay young
It remembers the days
That bells once rung
No matter our yearly age
We all hold memories of love within
Upon the hearts golden age
There forever we'll refresh
The love upon our hearts page
Now just remember
Someday you'll become a member
Of this exclusive book club
So ring those bells while yet you may
To store them in memory
For another day

Chapter Four
Holiday Poems

Thanks Giving Plate

On this Thanksgiving day
There are many that are alone and afraid
Many that have lost their jobs and their way
So on the plate I add a helping of sharing.
And beside it I put a heap of caring
Now then there should be understanding
Oh yes I see it , right beside the love
It was kinda hidden behind the faith
that was sending up the prayer to above
As the child whispered softly ...please and thank you God
I handed the plate to him just as I heard him
say..Amen
His mother looked up with tears in her eyes
and I knew..
the plate was filled.

Cast Your Bread Upon The Waters

Bonnie Ray

Gifts

There are gifts you can wrap
and gifts that make you want a nap
Gifts that are expensive and some that
are cheap
I have none of the above to give you
my friend

But these are for you to keep...
I give you my love always true
My friendship too,
Yes it will be there for you
A shoulder to cry on
When life's dreams are bygone
A hand to hold when nights are long and cold
Memories to reminisce when we grow old

Together in friendship we'll share these years
A smile for your lips and a kiss
to take away life's tears
Some gifts you just can't wrap

Just One More Time

It's been awhile since we spent Christmas together
So I thought I would write you this letter
You know I miss you still
And I guess I always will
We didn't get to say goodbye
You slipped away when I wasn't looking
Guess you didn't want to see me cry
All I have are the memories of our last Christmas we
spent
Seems like so long ago as I watched you open your gifts
I didn't know then, that all too soon, to heaven you
would be sent
I thought that , I had more time, but time moved far to
swift
I know someday soon we will meet again
But missing you keeps on hurting within
I'll put up the tree and do like always before
And I'll keep listening for your knock upon my door
Your place at the table I'll set as I do every year
Maybe if you aren't to busy in heaven
You can find time to visit dear
But if you can't make it, I'll understand
So many things to do and so little time
God had your day already planned
And I know you will be watching from above
With a smile on your face and a heart full of love

Bonnie Ray

But ohh ..what I would give for...
Just one more time

We miss you Ma

Remembering The Holidays

As the holidays approach ever near
I'm reminded of the days of yesteryear
Of the ones that will not be at the table
The ones we lost and held so dear
Now all thats left are tears and an empty place
But we are still holding the love in our hearts for them
And the memory of their dear face
With a prayer sent wish to see them again
Memories will be spoken around the table
As we each in turn recall the ones we loved
Sharing a story of the days gone by
With pain in our hearts and a tear in our eye
Memories we share of their favorite things
Like their favorite saying or their favorite pie
And how their laughter would ring
A tired old joke, that dad would tell every year
Or how great was Mama's cup of homemade cheer
Our brothers and sisters that came from far and near
As how on Sunday mornings their voices in praise
would ring out loud and clear
And we'll remain here with memories and love
While we remember the ones who've gone above
We again find ourselves..
Remembering the holidays

Bonnie Ray

The Good Old Days

There she sat at the piano playing those old songs
The ones that make you remember old hurts and wrongs
Her hands not quite as nimble as they once were
But still the melody was sweet and all her
A hundred times we had done this before
Our family tradition, to follow each year
The house would ring with laughter and good cheer
As we would celebrate the holidays
Together as a family... like always
The old piano is silent now
Sits lonely in the corner
The maestro has taken her final bow
Upon the desk a picture of her
We dust it daily to be sure
Sometimes in the silence of the night
I imagine I can hear her playing softly
The songs she loved with such delight
One night I thought I heard her playing
You Are My Sunshine..
I got up to see but the piano was silent
And there was nothing but old memories, left behind
Perhaps the strains I heard had drifted from on high
And she was just , playing on a cloud , drifting by

My Christmas Prayer

Now I lay me down to rest
I pray Dear Lord you see
I've done my best
Upon this holy night I ask
That others to will be blest
A soldier will return safe
from his duties far away
Guide and protect by night and day
The homeless will be found a home
With no more need to roam
The sick returned to health
and those poor will find their wealth
A heart found broken ,in need of love
will find a mending Angel,
You have sent from above
No lonliness will be found
Love Hope Joy Faith Prosperity
Throughout the world abound
Around the world Peace will reign
We ask this In Your Heavenly name
Amen

Bonnie Ray

Pictures From The Past

Today I came across the past
Neatly tucked inside a yellow envelope
Placed there pictures to preserve and last
The years ago I put them there
was then my ' present' for this future time
Not ever dreaming then
I'd write those memories in a rhyme
A photo of me and grandaughter aged three
How she did shine..
that sweet angel.... then of mine
Married now, with angels of her own.
I hear from her, sometimes... by phone.
A photo of an old car..
One I owned .....was my hearts desire
Would out run anything on the road by far
And then I saw the pictures of dad
All dressed in his tuxedo for your wedding
I can still hear his words to your hubby
Saying Son..do you kno what a jewel your getting
Oh yes...and there is aunt Ruth on her walker
At 87 she still was quite a talker
Her greatest thrill... was cheating at poker
These memories and pictures
The stories they tell
Why look... there is one of me
Ringing that old dinner bell

I remember that summer in the garden
Roses bloomed that year ..so beautifully
These pictures from the past
mean so much to me
Funny how they become....
Such a wonderful 'present' to last
Now that the silver has twined the gold
All these pictures from the past
have such stories to be told

Bonnie Ray

Boogie Woogie Gal

She was only five foot two
But she could play that boogie woogie true
Her fingers across that keyboard flew

Out in the street,
The neighbors were dancing
to her boogie woogie beat

Anytime you had a request
Step up and ask
She would give you her best

Never had a piano lesson
Not a note had she read
Boogie Woogie Gal

Born with it all in her head
Life of every party
Sweet Boogie gal
Get down hearty

Made you tap your feet
Grab your partner
Get down with that boogie beat
Boogie Woogie gal played all night long
Come daylight she'd still be going strong

Xmas Knot

I am so tired of being alone
When the holidays come
There's nobody to invite home
When the snow flies
and the wind howls the fire flickers
There's only memories of sad goodbyes

So tired of smiling and trying to be gay
While others around me
all laugh and play

I'm cold and lonely ..
in a place that's dark and dreary
With no one to hold me ,
Or call me dearie

Friends wave from afar
Send cards and ask how I are
So hard to say I 'm fine
When I am so lonely all the time
Holidays come and go ..
Only the lonliness stays
Each years passing slow
And so am I ..

Bonnie Ray

While I sit and remember
some long ago goodbye

Christmas music rings far and wide
Santas on the corners ringing bells
But still there is no one by my side
Each old soul has their own private hells

Once upon a time in a land far away
I trimmed a tree and wrapped the presents
Then danced all night till light of day

But that was a long ago yesterday
Now my stomach is tied in a knot
Presents from loved ones
That are gone but not forgot

They're the ones I haven't got
Invisible just like the tree
Only seen by me

But felt in the form of a
Xmas Knot

Be My Valentine

*My sweetest friend on this day of love
I send you this card
Because I know God sent you from above
As a special Angel that watches over me*

*You worry about me
if I don't show up on time
And each night you wish me sweet dreams
As we say goodnight and sign off line
So I made this card just for you*

*Attached is my love as always
Bound with a ribbon of lace
to let you know our friendship
is special and we can never replace
What God has given by His grace*

Chapter Five
Nature

Swans Of Love

Upon the rivers mirrored glass
In shadowed perfection
A beauty of extreme class
Her long neck in regal poise
She glides on her perfect home
Left all alone nowhere to roam
Since her mate had been taken
She remembered that day in grief
Her soul to the roots were shaken
Now she glides alone with only her memories
Someday maybe she will find another
But for now she longs for ...no other
Mated for life these swans of love
Just like it is written above

Bonnie Ray

Marshmallow Crème

In the dusk of evening I drove the ribbon of highway
home
On an old country road, that I loved to roam
Alongside of the road the trees were covered in snow
A road of fairytale beauty like being in a marshmallow
creme world
And I felt like it was my own private slide show
Every branch covered, even the ones knotted as in
beaded purl
Huge branches of pine and spruce hung heavy with fresh
white clumps
as if coated by huge white marshmallows that melted in
lumps
The reflection of my headlights upon the trees made them
shimmer
in icing of white flocking of fairy land glimmer.
Around a curve I saw a deer in graceful exit as he
crossed the road
Such a wondrous creature in beauty so graceful in
fleeting flight
The night wind rushed past my car like a giant
stalking and
singing a wistful song of an enchanting forest delight
The miles were a journey of pearlescent night fall
A kodak memory to hold......... for future recall

Soon my journey would end and my ride thru the fantasy land
Would bring me back.... to the city , of man
Where the streets were covered in dirty slush and smog
The smells of pollution and the factories that clog
Where dreams the dreams of the American dream
And my heart yearned once again for the pristine beauty
of a ribbon that sparkled with marshmallow creme

Bonnie Ray

September's Flame

Summers Passing Glance
Another summer passing in review
Soon the leaves will flame
In multicolored hue
And the wind shall come to play her game
Clutching at me and you
When all of summers memories
Shall carry us the winter through
In flaming embers we rake ..
the colors of Septembers flame
Such beauty my breath it does take
Brings the artist brush to fame
While in summers fading glory
Flowers leave behind dried stems
to tell the age old story
Reminding us they were our friends
that once brought beauty to our lives
And they shall return again as summer begins
But for now they wait for winters winds
Summer fades much like a sunset closes
To rest in winters white repose

Gentle Summer Rain

A gentle summer rain
Reminds me of you,
And all the sweet things you do
Like the flowers you give to me
when you know my day was bad
The candlelight dinners shared
and all the laughter we had
Holding hands,strolling along the beach
as the sunset bids farewell to day
We watch it sink just out of reach
Like children we were back then
With love to share... drifting through
life........ just me and you.
Now I glance.... and see you smiling too
as you remember , and caress those moments
we have shared, like children...at play.
How much I love you so..
perhaps... you will never know.
The years have been kind to us
and silver has streaked our hair
But our love still remains intact
Held in our hearts, to share,
On a warm summer day....
In gentle summer rain

Bonnie Ray

Petals Of Life

Rose petals drift to the ground
As the night wind kisses softly
Nary a sound..so silently
Each has fulfilled it's life
Stars fall from heaven, make a wish quickly
Dream a dream ,live it into reality
Love someone ...with all your heart
Tell them everyday ...
Because life is fleeting away
For we are as the rose petals
So beautiful and gone all too soon
And the circle completes again
Beneath God's glorious moon

Chapter Six
Humor And Things

Ohh Sweet Sugar Daddy

Ohh.. Sugar Daddy Mine
Sweet Sugar Daddy mine
You are my loving honey
Taste so sweet and divine
You are mine all mine
Long and lean,
never are you mean
Some say you are square
But to me ..you're always fair
Spoil me with delight
Each and every night
Ummm....let me hold you tight
Make me lick my lips
Sooner or later...
you'll embrace my hips
Ohhh, sweet sugar daddy mine
You are so fine
Love you like nobodys loved you
I'll forever be true
Cause I sure love you
Ohh my, Sugar Daddy
Why you are shrinking!
Now look out there,
What were you thinking?
No no...not that sugar daddy kind
Even though they are nice

Bonnie Ray

But oh so hard to find
Mine I like to keep on ice
Ohh Sugar Daddy ,my candy bar
The sweetest one to me by far
Gotcha!

Laughing Breeze

I pick a leaf from the trees
And gently toss it, with my breeze
I tug on your garments
And I kiss your cheeks

Playfully I'll snatch your hat
Sending it into flight
I watch and laugh as you chase it with a wail
Ha ha ha, you better watch that skirt tail
Upon the waters I'll dance
Kissing the canvass sails to enhance
Swirling and twirling
Like lovers in sweet romance
Then I"ll lay low for awhile
as I watch you smile..you're thinking I'm gone
But not for long, I will return
To ruffle your hair ..ah yes
You"ll know I'm there
I'm the laughing breeze
Coming back to tease

Bonnie Ray

Song Of The Sea

Sing to me your song of yesterday and today
Remind me of my childhood day
Where once upon your sandy beaches I built
castles and dreams.

Sing to me your peaceful melodies
So I may be the child again
in natures harmonies

Lay at my feet your treasures of deep
give me melodies of your song to keep
Sing to me your song of yesterday and today
Remind me of my childhood way

Wishin' Fishin'

Well here I sit just a wishin'
I twas afishin'
But the grass needs mowed
and the clothes needs sewed
Down at the lake, that ole catfish is jumpin
he makes my heart go athumpin
I sit and wish I could catch that dang fish
He would look so fine upon my dish
For today I guess will be a dream
And I'll put off my trip, down to the stream
Soon ol' friend, we'll meet again
I'll catch you in the end
Can't always keep amissin'
Until then... I 'll be wishin'fishin'.

Bonnie Ray

Little Jake And The Mouse

Little Jake saw a mouse
when he went to visit grandma's house
He watched that mouse go to and fro
Watched that mouse wherever he did go.
Mouse ran under the cabinet and stove
around the table and beneath the fridge
Skittering and scattering upon the floor
running here and there but not out the door.
Well granny squealed and Jake laughed with glee
As granny said ..Quick Jake
Hand that broom to me
Jake gave granny the broom
and she chased that mouse from room to room.
Tricky lil mouse ..I'll get you yet
On that lil mouse, you can bet
For out the door into the snow
on this very day you will go.
Well the race went on until down went the sun
Granny was plumb tuckered out
She had to rest awhile because of her gout
Jake says Granny can I keep him please
I'll feed him everyday lots of cheese
Granny says... my goodness child
Not a mouse in my house for a pet
They are cute now... but they get big
and will eat like a pig.

Soon the house was quiet and the mouse
resumed his running riot
Too late he knew.. cause Granny had him by the tail
She set a trap along his trail
Jake was sad because the mouse had to go
As granny tossed the mouse out into the snow
Granny felt bad because Jake was sad
so the next day to the pet store they went
Jake was happy as a lark
Cause when they came home and opened the cage
His new pet gave a happy little bark
Jake had a new friend,
And Granny was happy to again

Bonnie Ray

Tweety's Revenge

Yeah Yeah good morning..
I'm on my way to my PC
To see just what you mailed me

I've tamed dat puddy tat dis morning
Put him on my feet as you see

Caught him while he was sleeping
Now don't wook at me like dat
You know he would do da same to me
Cause he's a bad ol puddy cat

Ohhh I see, MaryFrances and Granny
Emailed me
Looking in every nook and cranny
Saying they can't find Sly
Wonder why they askin Tweety
My my... why oh why

Shh don't tell them, we know don't we
Early bird gets da wurm
But I made dat puddy tat squirm

He He He

Tweety And Puddy Tat

Puddy tat puddy tat
Let me show you where it's at
I told U and I told U
No mess with that
Leave my little tail alone
I'm gonna tell on you
And Granny will make you blue
Her little broom
Will send you to your room
Soon you gonna meet your day of doom
Sly you gonna go bye bye
And I not gonna cry cry
So leave my lil' tail alone
Or Granny gonna find you a new home
Remember last time i wore you on my feet
This time I ain't gonna be so sweet
I will tie your tail over the clothesline
And you gonna whine whine whine

Bonnie Ray

My America

Across the land we call America
Amber waves of grain stand
To sustain us and those in foreign land
America...home of the open hand
The land of plenty always shares
Lady with a heart that cares
Ignorance tries hard to dim her light
But her flag waves..forever bright
Proudly she stands tall,
rising above the rubble, always there
To answer the call
When others in trouble, she never cowers
Not even when anger and hate.
topple her towers
Nor when grief comes like a thief
trying to steal her belief
Her Majesty stands ..
and rings the bell of freedom
Throughout her lands, from sea to sea
She will forever be ...
the crown jewel of liberty
My America..built by forefathers hands
 in faith hope and love and guidance from above

God Was Suspended

Remember when prayer in schools
Was a part of the rules
Along with
The pledge of allegiance
From the beginning of school
It was a teachers daily tool
As well as the golden rule
Then came the day
When they decided
We didn't need to pray
They sent God away
With a failing grade
Satan enrolled..
With his set of rules
And the bells of hell tolled
Kids think he is so cool
Now the kids carry a gun or blade
And in the distance,
The Ten Commandments fade
They never heard the Lords prayer
Can't recite the pledge
Something is wrong there
Can;t read or write
Now in the street gangs fight
Earphones and rap and hip hop
Violence that does not stop

Bonnie Ray

Drug dealers on the corner
Waiting for the next victum
To hook, badger and garner
No time for school
Or the Golden Rule
Off to the mall and
shop till they drop
Spending...
Hard earned money
From Mom and Pop
Christmas is coming
Shall we buy them a gun?
Will a teacher or child die
Before the next rising sun?
Sorry folks...
This is the truth
Wake up congress!!
Do we need more proof?

Homeless Winters

The winters snow covers the earth
A blanket of soft white
In the night... moments.....
Bear heavily the sound of silence
We ponder in solitude our self-worth
While around the world in various places
Life is given and taken....
In those same moments
A million others of unknown faces
Some come and go......
Without leaving traces
No footprints......
Left behind in the snow
I sit and I listen...
To the silence,
And ponder..where did all
Those unknown faces go

Bonnie Ray

Satan's Summer Dream

Long hot summer days
Long... sultry nights
Bright lights,city ways
Lots of ..gang fights
Sirens.. are blaring
A child ..is crying
No one ..is caring
Someones...buying
Distant.. shotgun blast
A mothers child.. is dying
See them ...run fast
Please ...we pray
Help us ...Father
Please ...don't say
You.... won't bother
Peace on earth..
Today... it's not found
What price ...it's worth
Earth keeps spinning round

Little Boy Grown Tall

Oh how you put on such a show
With your scrowl and grumpy voice
Trying to hide the real you I know
Would you believe, you have no choice
Because... I see inside your heart
Deep inside where your smiles are kept
You're just a teddy bear playing a part
Hiding away the tears you've wept
Don't be afraid, to love again
I 'll take your sadness away
We'll hold hands and dream new dreams
Together we'll find the bright new day
As we travel through life's rivers and streams

Bonnie Ray

Little Blue Angel

Little bit of Angel
and a little bit of devil
But mostly Angel
Can't seem to keep her wings level
Always falling from the sky
Earth is always a hard landing
She was never taught how to fly
Life is always demanding
For this little blue angel
Sits alone and crys
She makes her apologies
for her blunders
Always wanting to please
But the lil devil on her shoulder
demands her to tease
Go ahead be a little bolder
he taunts ..
Just this once forget others wants
Take a break, have some fun
So she did ...
And now in trouble again
But before she was done
this is what she did
She put that lil devil on the run
Brushed him right off her shoulder
on his tush ..Shwoosh

and she asked
How's that for bolder?
Now the little blue Angel
can fly right up to the sky
Cause she told the lil devil
bye bye

Bonnie Ray

Somebody's Daughter

On a corner on the streets of America
Stands a Gypsy Child searching for love
Gypsy child somebody's daughter
Once was an angel sent from above
Sweetness washed away
cause mama forgot her
Gypsy child , Gypsy child runaway
Will you be here on another day

No more fields of flower or clover
Only memories to remind you
Thirteen seasons behind you
A million reasons to blind you

Somebody's daughter Gypsy child
Combs her hair and paints her lips
Then off to the corner she slips
On the corners of America

Gypsy child cries as the snow falls deep
Gypsy child O Gypsy child
Tonight ...where will you sleep
Thirteen seasons left behind
A million reasons so unkind

Somebody's daughter
O mama , mama,
Why have you forgot her

--

Bonnie Ray

The Poet Voices Impressions

From the pen the Poet will strike your heart
Words that will inflict emotion you can't control
Impressions given are the readers role
Mind pictures you percieve, may be worlds apart
Fiction , truth, humor, sadness,insight, wisdoms, true
love,
Poets pen ,such power it wields by day and night
Whither come the words written?.
Subjects revealing ,appealing, concealing
From the paper of life a Poets bitten
Reading the words, as they form their quiet impressions
Depiction of all the worlds plight
Poets send forth their expressions
While giving the reader multiple choices
And thus... the Poet voices

Modern Technology

Have you ever tried to use your printer
And much to your surprise
The well was dry
Have you ever tried to fill it?
When you had no clue
As to just how to do
Let me tell you friends,
If it were not for the ink upon my carpet
On my legs, hands and feet
I'd grab a hammer and give this dang thing a whammer
But for now it's bleach and towels
Cussing and scowls
Next time I'll call the PC Doctor
And he can prescribe the remedy
Or better yet the junkman to get this piece of...
Modern technology!

Bonnie Ray

Computer Games Of Love

While Surfing along one fine day.
A room of Love I found.
Unknowingly of their way.
Rules of truth are unbound.
I thought , here I will linger .
Why there's even a singer
A moments pleasure this.
I am such a naive Miss.
Names of girls and boys.
Hopes dreams and joys.
A fleeting moment of chivalry.
Often ends up in rivalry.
A kiss maybe a hug or two.
Broken hearts that are blue.
Lots of hello's and goodbyes.
Many questions of why oh why's.
So the moral is, if you surf.
Be very careful of the turf.

Music Box Dancer

Upon the shelf in my room,
sits an old friend in darkened gloom.
Enclosed in her tiny little room.
Until I open the lid , and see her dance and twirl
She never holds a grudge when I stay away to long
This little friend, this tiny little girl
Sweet are the notes of her little song
Her cheerful little heart sings all the while.
Many times she made me giggle and smile
Brightened my day or my night
Made me happy and made me glad
Whenever opened... she pops into my sight
Bringing memories of days of delight
When Mama would sit her beside my bed
And turn on my nightlight
After my prayers I had said
The music would play on and on
As off into dreams I went
to play,with the Angels..that,
Heaven had sent

Chapter Seven
Short Stories

Bonnie Ray

Where The Peonies Bloom

Upon an old winding country road I took that drive once more.

The old road has seen many changes, since I first traveled it.

Every year I take that short trip to where the peonies bloom.

Along the road the scenery has changed from corn fields and woods,where all manner of wild life once ran free.The farms are gone now replaced by high priced mansion type homes.

There used to be an old wooden covered bridge that I had to cross. This old bridge used to give me chills as a child. I could hear it creak and moan as the car rolled over the wooden planks.I would silently pray that I wouldn't wind up in the creek. Here in Indiana we have many beautiful old wooden bridges some have been renovated and some closed off to traffic but still accessible by foot.

The day was sunny and a light spring breeze blew in the open windows of my car in fragrant earthy aromas., as I passed a small old farm that had managed to survive that thing we call progress.

In the field adjacent to the old farm house , a few mares and their new colts frolicked in the sun.

Each time the wind freshened the colts would take off in playful romp. So beautiful in their running gait. Like a picture postcard. Across the rolling green field, their short

little tails fanned out in the wind as their long legs raced
the wind.

As I neared the gates where the peonies bloom , I could
see them on the hill tall and stately in full bloom,
They had spread since last year and completely covered
the tombstone. Beautiful pinks in various shades of
blossoming beauty. Yellow and purple irises mingled
at the base of the peonies, Poor mans orchids my
grandmother always called them. She and I had planted
them there many years ago, on my mothers grave. I was
only 8 at the time. Now she to rests where the peonies
bloom. The memories I have of the times we used to go
there to decorate

the graves. Usually my cousin Terry and my aunt were
with us. Terry and I loved to run through the cemetery
playing hide and seek. He would always run ahead and
hide and then jump out at me as I ran past his hiding
place. Scared the daylights outta me because he was
always Dracula and going to suck my blood. Our TV fare
was mighty limited back then. And the worse thing that
could happen to you was Dracula or the Zombies getting
you. We used to roam all over that old cemetery looking
at the dates on the tombstones and making up stories
about the old ones. Some dated back to 1849.

I parked my car along the lane about even with my
mothers resting place, got out and walked up to the site.
The fragrance of the peonies greeting me like a sweet
warm hug and kiss of an old friend. I cut the weeds

*and placed the wreaths I had brought for the 3 graves ,
said my prayers and goodbyes. Someday.... I too will rest
there.... where the peonies bloom.*

Bonnie Ray

Little Nellie

Little Nellie
Little Nellie
With a pot belly,
Not much bigger than a jar of jelly
Fell in the butter churn,
And couldn't turn.
No way could she get out!
A cry for help upon her lips,
Ma...Ma..I done slips
Well Ma came running to help Little
Nell in her moment of distress
She wrung her hands in her apron dress,
As she sang out loud S.O.S.
They came from far and near
To help Little Nellie dear
Poor child was crying in fear
As they twisted and turned
Little Nell in the churn
Lots of words of ..Oh gosh durn
For stuck she was,in the antique churn!
With great regret..
They knew they would have to it break
If Little Nell they were to unset
Authors Note:
This is a true story.
Happened to a dear old friend when she was a child
She is now passed on at the age of 89 .
Dedicated to the memory of Nellie Herald
 whom we loved
And called Mama Nellie.

Uncle John's Rooster

Many years ago when I was a child I remember a cabin in
Tennesee
Where Uncle John and Aunt Mabel lived
A pair of gentle nature.He worked his fields with a plow
and mules.
Aunt Mabel canned and cleaned without modern tools.
A well they had for water.Carried in from outside in
buckets.
An old wood cook stove,where Aunt Mabel did the best
meals-
Food that melted in your mouth
Every night before bed me and Uncle John,
 had cornbread and buttermilk in a bowl or glass.
Uncle John was my idol in case you haven't guessed
Now Aunt Mabel had an old rooster
That hated the world,me included.
Every chance he got,he would chase me around the lot
and peck or flog me,with his wings.
You see I was only about 4 years old at the time
I wanted to be friends,but he wasn't in the mood..ever!
One day I went outside to play and I heard Aunt Mabel
say
be mindful of that rooster child, I said ok as I went out
the door.
Uncle John had gone to town, to get supplies and have
the corn ground.

Well I loved to explore, so off I went. You see in the
country there is always a new place to look for, a
Veritiable fairy land to a child of four.
Sometimes I would go down to the pond to give the ducks
that lived there some cornbread. But today I went to the
barn instead, I loved the smell of the hay
and the cows.
 I knew all by name, Joey an Jack the two mules
were there too.
Sometimes , Uncle John put me up on their backs to ride
Back to the barn after he got done plowing. Well, you
might know, on this particular day
That danged rooster was up in the hay. When I spied him
I
knew it was time to make tracks to the house, just as
fast as my little legs could get me there.
I took off just a flyin yellin' for Aunt Mabel all the way, I
got almost to the house and stubbed my toe, down I went
and I knew I was gonna get it.
Here come Old Joe the rooster, wings a flapppin and
jumping like a rabbit.
Well me and Old Joe was agoin at it, him a peckin and
me a swattin,
when I heard the sound of Uncle John's old car in
the drive, I gave a yell and he came running with a stick
in his hand,
a determined look on his face, I knew Old Joe had met
his match.

I was sure glad to see Uncle john.
Well aunt Mabel grabbed me up, took me in the house an
patched me up, sat me down in her lap and read me a
story.
I fell asleep, and when I awoke to the fine smell of Aunt
Mabel's cooking,
I knew I didn't have to worry bout Old Joe no more.
Now they have both gone on , but I will always
remember
Uncel John and the rooster.

Bonnie Ray

Angel In Waiting

Everyday she sat by the window and watched and waited. Searching each face as the person came walking up the sidewalk. Like a child at Christmas, sifts through the presents for that one special package. Anticipation upon her face would turn to a frown as they got close enough for her to see them clearly. Bound to that wheel chair, unable to walk on her own, each day she would whisper to (herself) it's almost time .. it's almost time. Sometimes when she was overheard the nurse would ask her ...what is almost time Serepta? To which she would reply, to get my wings , to get my wings so I can fly away home. Her silvered hair glistened as the sunlight streamed into her room. The walls were bare except for a faded picture of a young man, whose name if you should ask her, she could not recall.

Upon her bed a coverlet of many colors, the nurses thought might brighten up her room. She never had any visitors except for the Sisters Of Mercy, from the convent. Her eyes would light up as she reached for the package they brought, knowing that inside she would find that sweet confection she craved. Her tiny fingers tore open the bag and she reached inside for a gum drop. She selected a red gum drop and plopped it into her mouth, as the sweetness embraced her taste buds a look of pure delight spread across her face. Looking for all the world

like a small wrinkled child.
With a nod of thanks she turned back towards the
window, to continue her vigil. Another ritual completed
just as all the other times in the past seven years that she
had been a resident here at the nursing home.

No one could seem to remember how Serepta came there,
least of all her. It was as if she had just always been
there. The nurses that used to work there seven years
ago had retired or moved on to other jobs. The day shift
would bathe and feed her each morning and put her in her
wheel chair to sit by the window. Not that she couldn't
have gone into the day room with the other residents, but
because it was her preference to sit by the window. The
nurses had tried to wheel her into the day room on several
occasions but, she caused such a fuss it was much easier
and quieter to let her stay by the window. After supper
the night shift would put her gown on her and give her
the medication she required and place her in her bed.

The days drew near to Christmas and the nursing home
was being
decorated for the holidays. Hustle and bustle of nurses
coming and going echoed though the halls on a daily
basis. Music would drift down the hall from an ancient
radio played by the resident old joker, named Bill.

He was able to wander the halls on his own, and occasionally find his way
into visit the other patients.
His favorite hideaway to visit was in Serepta's room, she was always there at her window watching. Once he asked her what it was she was looking for ... to which she replied...my wings. Serepta was not one to talk, quite content to be left alone with her vigil. That suited Bill just fine as he could sit and talk and tell his tales of his younger days without being interrupted. Secretly Serepta listened to his ramblings. Once Bill could have sworn, he saw a glimpse of a smile, during one of his tall tales.

Finally Christmas Eve arrived and as usual everyone was in a rush to get things ready for visiting day tomorrow. The aromas wafting down the halls from the kitchen seemed to put everyone in a jolly good mood. As they anticipated the dinner they would get tomorrow. Old Bill was ambling through the halls with his cane, loudly wishing all within ear shot ,Merry Christmas ho ho ho. A rather loud shout came from a distant room telling Bill to shut-up you dang fool , it's the middle of July! Bill grinned and continued on his way to Sereptas' room to say hello and wish her a Merry Christmas . As he entered her room he noticed that her wheelchair was empty!
He looked around to see if she might be in her bed but,

no she wasn't there either. He rushed off to the nurses station to ask where she might be.

Lisa, the head nurse, was busy doing the charts when Bill excitedly began firing questions at her about Serepta. She put down her clip board and said, whoa there Bill, now what's the problem dear? It's Serepta he cried, where is she ? Why she is in her room Bill , I just checked on her. No No , Bill exclaimed , she is gone I looked and she isn't there. Come along Bill I ' ll show you she is there , said Lisa. As they entered the room and saw the empty wheelchair , Lisa went to check the bathroom and found it empty.

As she approached the old wheelchair she couldn't believe what she found in the seat of the chair..a tiny white feather....

To this day no one mentions Sereptas name, except old Bill , he scratches his head everytime he walks past that empty room.

The nurse Lisa , went on to another facility, after being dismissed for losing a patient.

Oh by the way....if you should meet an Angel named Serepta, tell her Lisa said hello.

Bonnie Ray

Angel In Cotton Print

As I walked down the corridor I saw her sitting there
She was looking for someone to speak or to care
I knew not her name or from where she came
But the joy on her face as I approached was priceless
She grabbed my arm and tried to speak
In her mind .....I... was the one she did seek
I could tell she'd had a stroke
No way could I understand all the words she spoke
But one of the things I understood her to say
Was...... do you know ME?
Pretending that I did ....
I hugged her and told her how pretty she looked
While I listened to her joy and watched the light in her
eyes
As she babbled on like a sparkling brook
And prayed to heaven God Bless this poor soul
With the bluest of eyes as bright as the skies
Her hair shone like silver and her dress was of cotton
print
She reminded me of an Angel
That was Heaven sent
Whose wings had been clipped
As I gently told her goodbye and continued on my way
Thinking to myself......
God spoke to me that day

Chapter Eight
Loss And Grief

Just Beyond The Blue

Just beyond the blue..is whereI've gone
Shed no tears..for I wait for you here
I'm just beyond the blue of God's glorious day
There is no more pain for me
My Lord took it all away
Though you cannot see my face
I am nearby always
Remember I still love you
And I am ..
Just beyond the blue

Bonnie Ray

And I still Miss Someone

Something is missing
Could it be me
Or is it you?
A piece of my heart is gone
I do believe it is true

Heartbeat is irregular
Pulse barely beating

Look there's a tear
My heart is weeping

Something is missing
Could it be me?
Or is it you?

Crossing Jordan

I held your hand and felt you leave
While I alone was left to grieve
Someday we will meet again
I know you...
will be there to welcome me in
When time for me to come
and my life here on earth is done
Once again we will be as one
Until that day.. I know you walk beside me
I hear your voice in the wind
Whispering ....
I miss you my friend

Bonnie Ray

Journey's End Prayer

The old one took a seat upon the ground
And began his prayer in humble sound
Creator Of All
Hear my prayer..
I am so old and tired,my children are grown
And have all left home.
I am now alone And wish to come Home
My life I have lived to this age
And I have written my lifes page
I hope and pray with kindness
Look upon my heart and hear my plea
There you will find me
My lifes song I have sung in the sun
Trying to be the man you said we should be
I thank you Great Spirit for my life
For the good times and the strife
They made me who I am
You gave me a wonderful life
All the good things are gone now
My wife ,my children,my youth
You blessed me well
And I am greatful, thats truth
No longer are my sunsets as beautiful
My eyes cannot appreciate fully their beauty
Only in my heart,,do I hear the songbird sweetly

Not Just Another Woman

To the world I am only just another woman
But to the ones I love and who love me I am much more
The world sees me as just another woman
Others eyes will view me as the one they adore
A few will think I am more than just one
To them I have wings of an angel on their days of need
For I always hear their cry of sorrow, hurt and pain
And rush to soothe and ease their sorrow in speed
Many will know me by many names
Never forgetting my touch
Remembering me as one of the great dames
Forever knowing I loved them so much
I'm always easy to find
Since I am everywhere you look
No need to stress your mind
Or search the address book

My name is...Woman ,
Daughter Sister
Cousin Aunt,Friend
Wife ,Mother and
Grandmother
I bet you know one to
that's
Not...
just another woman

Bonnie Ray

Dedicated to the women of the world
And some I know personally
are,
Not..Just Another Woman

Remnant In My Heart

In my heart are the
remnants of my broken dreams
Pieces of you saved from yesterday
Where once there were reams
A bit of a beautiful sunset..
a remembered rainbow
that followed the rain
The favorite song to me you sang
still echos softly the melody
A mental image of the sketch you
did of me from a picture you sent
The hours and days of laughter we spent
When our hearts were in harmony
and we could reach across the span of miles
sharing our hearts and smiles
These remnants I will cherish
Time will not erase them
For I will not let them perish
Like a hand carved pattern on a piece of art
I'll retrace them ,the remnants in my heart.

Bonnie Ray

Judge Me Not

For...
Loving you
I had no choice
Even knowing ...
You might... make me blue

Someday you may find
The love I hold for you
Has always been..
The truest of true

If another has your heart
And that keeps us apart
Then I wish you both the best

But honey... please don't say
This is a test
The day... I met you
I knew I had been blest

Even tho... I may never
Hold you close, or hear you say
You love me too
Please remember my heart
Once belonged to you

And if some day....
I walk thru your mind
Remember.... I loved you
As though I were blind

So judge me not for
Loving you....
Judge me only ...
For being a fool

Bonnie Ray

Black Of Night

In black of night when all was still
I felt his presence enter the room
And it gave me pause and chill
A gust of air as cold as ice
Filled the room and my heart
Fate had rolled the dice
My love to soon.. to depart
Cancer won.....death it's price
I knew he would come, to bring his doom
Knew all to well when he entered the room
He lingered and stalked in corners dark and drear
Ever closer he approched to steal the hearts beat
He had come to take away my darling dear
To beg and plead upon my knees twould be for naught
Away into the night he rode upon his black steed
My darling's soul caught within his grasp..
His fated mission accomplished in record speed
I shall ne'er forget the pain he left behind
As he left with my darling mine
No more the songbird shall I hear
but I will think of.... my darling dear
To remember his laughing eyes ,so like the sky of blue
Throughout our life we shared and loved
ne'er doubt his heart for me ...was ever true
Now upon an evening's breeze I hear his loving sighs
Perhaps a sweet moment.... of once more goodbyes

Beneath the stars high above or upon the moors of yore
Someday my love we'll meet again on the distant shore
And ne'er part..... never more

Bonnie Ray

Garden Of Flowered Regret

To visit the garden of regret
and drink from the well..
Grasp the vines of memory
and enter therein to hell
Vines withered and sere
of rememberance in fear
And dine on essence of yesteryear
Showers of ashes awash the hope
and drown anew the sprigs that grope
As gasping for breath of tomorrow
Now succumbs to sorrow..
Splashing tears in heat of passion lost,
begs to be paid by yesterdays cost

Love Life And Death

Love, Life and Death walk hand and hand
It is but a moment in time... A breath away....
Which hand you decide to take
For only your soul or your heart
that decision can make
Whether you take the hand of life and live
Or walk the path of death and never give
Many times the choice is yours
Death comes in many disguises
Lonliness is one of it's best guises
For it leads one to believe it lives
And keeps it's secret so beguilingly
As we trip thru life daily

To walk in sunshine and take a chance on life
Or walk in silence deep across the death moors
Life and love can breathe or die
By half truths or a simple lie
One heart left alone to cry
Two hearts in same tempo never meet
To ever know.. if maybe......or even,
Why
Ignoring what we do not understand
Maybe it will disappear
As this is sometimes our ways
Letting it become a part of old yesteryday
This is too true I fear

Bonnie Ray

Look To Heaven

O how I long for the innocence of yesterdays
Back before hate and evil destroyed childrens dreams
Before Humankind discovered evil ways
And devised the means... to enact it's schemes
Yesterdays I remember with warm heart
When poets words thrilled with paletted scenes
And artists brush, stroked the clock, of times part
Days when a handshake was the only accepted bond
Where love ,life and pursuits of happiness, ruled the days
Seeds of hope sewn.. now ripped up.. by hands that
abscond
To remember these days of innocent yester ways
Oh.....of these I am most fond
Of days that drifted once on golden pond
This now the bread of man,   is made from old leaven
Spoiled by the fermenting of greeds unrepenting
Now nothing left but ...to look to heaven

Faded Rose

A rose of gold
Warm word unfold
Left me standing alone and cold
Man of love, was he
Why did he lie to me
Was it meant to be
Questions ...
Will I care again
A rose of paper
Pink glowing candle taper
Green eyes cry and love does die
Left behind are the wondering words
Why?
Heart of golden glass shattered
A life left in tatter
Does love really matter

Bonnie Ray

And When I Die

And when I die
Let it be spring
Place my bed at window sill
So I may hear the robins sing
And the sweet whip o will
Let it be Sunday as the church bells ring

Give me a gentle spring rain
To wash away the pain
As I leave behind memories
Of earths sweet refrain

The Shopping Cart

I look around my old town
And see what I found
There on the street
I see an old woman walking
Barely shoes on her feet
To herself she is talking
No place to lay her head
This old person
no home with a bed
Pushing that shopping cart
Worldly possesions inside
Where is the world with a heart
Did it run and hide
Let's open the doors wide
Perhaps we can help more outsiders
Why not?
We are the richest country in the land
I always heard charity begins at home
It must have decided to roam
To flee to a foreign land
Since we have such a free hand
We must have sold the golden rule
The powers that be
Sold it to a cheaper fool

Bonnie Ray

Poverty's Child

Have you seen her?
She lives in our neighborhoods
Does not matter
If you live in the city or near the woods
She is the child alone
The one with sad mourning eyes
Looking for a loving home
The one with no goodbyes
Have you seen her?
The child that needs
An encouraging word
To give her wings for her imagination
 to fly like a bird
I bet if you look hard enough
She may even live under your roof
Have you seen her?
Povertys child the living proof

The Little Old House

The little old house sits alone
once it had a woman to call it's own
But circumstance took her away
Now the roof is sagging and the grass needs mowing
Windows dirty without light showing
The porch steps are cracked and weeds grow through
Now the little old house remembers and sighs
and wishes there were never any goodbyes
It remembers the soft sounds of humming
and food on the stove cooking
When company was coming
How it longs for the lilting laughter of family and
children playing
It remembers it's woman and the many times it heard her
praying
and her soft songs of lullaby and nursery rhymes
As it sits alone and remembers the good times
Thirtyfive years ... my how they did fly
and the wind in the willows ..why I do hear them cry
They must miss her as I do
If you were a little old house ..you would to

And The Angels Cried

As I serenely sat and watched
The tide roll in and kiss the shore
Your memory knocked softly
Once again upon hearts door
And the angels cried
A love so beautiful had died
Then I cast a white rose
Upon a sea of blue
For heaven only knows
Our love...
Once was true
And the angels cried
Now I watch in wonder
As the sunset kisses the sky
And I ask God...why?
Does love have to die
And the angels cried
Softly as one by one the stars
Began to shine
I knew the answer
For as long as..you are
In my heart,
You will always be mine
Love never really died
It just drifted away
Gently...like the tide

Bonnie Ray

Just One More Look

(Kentucky)
Across the blue sky
Streaked by sunrise
A gaggle of geese fly
Heralding a cheerful
Good morning to me
Aw-honk Aw-honk
As they leave the pond
Where white ducks glide
To fly upon a hill of blue green
And eat their morning fill
I gaze in wonder upon this scene
Never does it fail to thrill
In the fields the Angus grazing
cattle,as the cowbirds rise
In excited winded chatter
Breaking the mornings hushed silence
As the new born calves struggle
To find their place and suckle
Old pidgeons around the silo gather
In hopes of feast from grains scatter
In graceful beauty stand trees that sway
From gentle morning breezes play
Upon the morning air,the scent of new mown hay
Wafting across my mornings day
Barefoot with cofffee cup in hand

,I step upon this real fairyland,feeling the blue grass
Tickle the bottoms of my feet
As I listen to the birds so sweet
If this were my last day to spend upon this earth
I would choose this scene to be my last look
For it truly exists,not found in a book
And as the angel came to carry me home
I would ask for one more moment
To take...just one more look
At my old kentucky home

Bonnie Ray

Kentucky Rain

Alongside the roads of two lane blacktop
on old country roads one can see the beauty of green
rolling hills and wire fences entwined with orange
trumpet flowers and honeysuckle vines.
Sparkling streams of green and crystal meander through
the hills and
beneath the bridges that have withstood the test of times.
Fields of clover and wild flower abound
and on clear cool nights one can hear the distant bay of
hounds .
Kentucky ...a place of beauty beyond compare
Places some have never seen are still found there
Hollows and caves that run underground
upon this earth no footsteps have made a print or a sound
High above stretch the mountains and hills that are
kissed by the morning mists pass by in glorious review
like soldiers standing at attention
Summer clouds drift upon a lazy afternoon
looking much like ice cream scoops of vanilla dipped by a
spoon.
Trees dressed in their best finery of lacy green sway with
the breezes of impending rain. The sky begins to darken
as if a window shade has decended
and the tall grasses bend as if swept by a giants invisble
broom
Across the green pastures that are dotted by black Angus

and Quarterhorses
let out to graze and run with the winds , a pond of deep
water is occupied by cattle cooling themselves in the
shady bends.
Freshening wind and drops of life giving rain kiss away
the heat of the sun's blistering pain.
A rain of heaven sent relief that kisses the soul
while one is refreshed again and made to feel whole .
Time passes under the drenching rain and it begins to
slacken it's pace
Soon ....the rainbow will take it's place
An arc of prism colors stretches across the sky
giving one the feeling of a fantasy land so pleasing to the
eye
This is my Kentucky ....land steeped in rich history with
it's good times and bad. Old southern mansions and
gentility , southern hospitality, and many good times
there I've had.. A softer slower pace of living , where
people show their kindness and hearts that are giving .
Sunday church and Sunday dinners,
rocking on the front porch and listening to the summer
serenade of nature.
Rainbows and gentle rains, green fields and wide open
spaces in my thoughts
will always be winners.

So Help Us God

So help us God if we allow the powers that be
to do away with the Pledge of Allegiance
Where will Americas freedom then be?
If we are not 'One Nation Under God'
then who are we??
God is not below us but above
If we do not ..In God We Trust
then whom would you suggest?
I know no other..that could carry us through
the hard times and pass every test.
Should we kick 'OLD GLORY' out of school
and forget to teach the Golden Rule.?
From what direction would the children of the future
lead
If we allow evil to make us the fool
Should we not sing a song of praise
or say a prayer or that Grand Old Flag raise.
We the people of The United States have
done very well as One Nation Under God
And twas because In God WE Trust
That this land remains free.
We are who and what we are today
because our forefathers fought for the Flag
and the right to Pledge Allegiance
If this offends you or your child..
may I suggest..the door to hell...

will open wide it's gates
and welcome you... without the sound of Libertys Bell.
My country , sweet land of liberty
Oh say can you see
Where the ruling is taking you and me.
And by God , Under God and as I stand before God
I shall forever pledge my allegiance to the flag.
And when I hear the Star Spangled Banner,
I will stand and never let my spirits sag.
For I know The Lords Prayer by heart.
I learned it in school along with the Pledge Of
Allegiance.
Never shall I forget my country nor forget to do my part.
This is My constitutional right !
May God continue to bless us day and night.

Chapter Nine
Poems Of Collaboration

During my years as a writer I have been priviledged to share my pen with some of today's finest writers. Here is a collection of those gifted people and myself. All poems herein this chapter are used with their permission

Friendship's Note

A broken arrow we will never see
This friendship strong and true
Secrets locked within the wind
I share with you

One heart broken cries to you
Pain you try to ease
Kindness in suffering helps in so many ways
Truth spoken never lies

Wisdom is friendship
For it never dies
Values we place upon the earth
Placed in heaven before our birth

Friendship tied with a knot
Held strong binded without fear
I speak to you my friend,you listen
You are always there
Today I thought of you
and how much you mean to me
I looked inside my heart
and what did I see?
There's a X that marks the spot
I have reserved it for you
Like a buried treasure plot

Inside there is friendship love thats true
Memories of times of me and you
Life's roses, Dreams,good and bad
Sunshine ,Secrets , Hopes and Tears

Just a few of these things we have shared
down through these past years
So I wrote this note.. as a reminder
just in case sometime I'm not here
You'll know without a doubt, my friend
I always...loved and held you dear
My friend you are the X that marks the spot
in my heart. Where love and friendship resides
Written by Bonnie Ray and Floreann Cawley.

We Are Greatful

I often wonder and want more than I have
I suppose it is natural to feel this way
I have been blessed so greatly
Gifts unexpected given to me
Not material, but from God blessings I can see
To share my sorrow and joy with friends I love
To laugh and cry and be myself
Make one smile when they are sad
For my friends I am grateful, I am glad
I am grateful for this wonderful world
All of Gods colors that I see
Yet there are times I just forget
To whisper Thank You silently
So many things taken for granted
Eyes closed at night without a thought
Treasures from the Hands of God
Precious gifts that can't be bought
I am greatful for the simple pleasures
The bird's song and the stars above
A smile from a child, or friend
Good morning hugs, given by love
A cup of coffee and morning's glow
Friends that call just to say hello
All these simple pleasures
Given daily by His Grace
Are my greatful treasures
These things nothing can replace
Floreann Cawley Maryfrances Perez
Bonnie Ray

Grace

Sweet glory upon us this day
we dwell in this land and seek
Our destiny is to live in peacefulness
Along the way we stumble
But we are not alone
As we rise above our sorrows
reaching out and touching a heart
Along our long journey
sometimes we leave an imprint behind
It cannot be erased,
yet many try...
For we are all one being
destined to meet in the end

No matter how twisted my lifes road
Grace from above helps carry the load
I only hope to have left behind goodness
And the world will remember me..
As one who served with kindness
I pray my imprinted path has made the road
easier to travel for those that come behind
For we are all one being searching for..
Grace
By Floreann Cawley and Bonnie Ray

Friends Forever

Floreann

Sometimes things do not go right
We have our moods, but we never fight
When our heart breaks, or we feel blue
We are blessed we turn not to one
But two
These friends I have a gift from God
They are more than friends, they are love
Share their time and wisdom with me
I love them both as you can plainly see.

Bonnie

Friends .. but more like sisters of the heart
Each one in turn will give the other a part
We share our hopes and dreams
Laughter and loving sharing scenes
Everyone has their ups and downs
Moods we change to help the other
By our antics we act like clowns
Sisters and best friends three
How blessed I am to have them
They mean the world to me
Do I love them? You bet!
Better friends , you can't get

MaryFrances

These two are more than friends
I know they'll be there til the end
There are things that I may never have
But when I'm down, they are the salve
They fill my heart with joy and laughter
When times are hard and things fall apart
They are the nails, the tar and the mortar
Bringing each day a brand new start
To me they are my family and more
Bringing smiles and sunshine to my door

A Heart Without A Friend Is A Heart Without A
Melody

Majestic Weaver

You hold me in your hand
I seek peace and love
To acquire joy is my destination
The road ahead is long, but I am not alone
For many seek what I need
Many want what I love
A soul woven with many knots
Tenderly
Upon this cloth threads are placed
In the correct location
Tightly woven with love each one strong
A blanket of warmth is created
Wrapped in a myriad of color
Gentle persuasions
Guiding, comforting, soothing
Bound by human kindness
Woven with the sheerest of silks
Freely given to those in need
Lost, lonely, worn down by life's journey
Mending broken wings
Rebuilding faith
Thus it begins.......a new journey
From birth we become a strand
In the Master Weavers rainbow plan
We are each unique yet all woven in His design
Each strand woven by life's pattern divine

He wove each strand with love for comfort
Bound the ties that bind with enduring effort
Intwined each of the strands He wove in
forgiveness, mercy, understanding,and eternal
love and compassion .
Around the border He placed Angels
to gently guide around the curves
Knowing the journey we
embarked upon would be long and sometimes cold
Before we arrived at His threshold
Floreann Cawley MaryFrances Perez And Bonnie Ray

Remember Our Soldiers
And say a prayer for them

Could You Do It

Stay awake for hours and fight the enemy
Walk a foreign land built on sand
Watch your buddies die in agony
To protect you and their homeland

Could you do it?

Watch the children as they lay injured
Bleeding and dying
Praying truth will overcome the perjured
For their truth is hidden by the lying

Could you do it?

Kill or be killed by those just as scared
When you close your eyes to sleep
You dream of home and wonder how they fared

Every day and night the same
Steaming days and desert nights
Nothing changes in the war game
Just one more of many fire fights

Could you do it?

I'm just eighteen yesterday
And I have a job to do
So remember me when you pray
Me and my brothers are protecting you

Eighteen makes me a man
I got my letter from Uncle Sam
My Mama cries and prays to God
That I won't die on foreign land

I hope I live to father a child
To know the comfort of a wife
But for now my country needs me
Even if it takes my life

I remember words from old soldiers
Remembering the days gone by
How they fought for home and ol' glory
How their brothers died so she could fly

I suit up for this war in sorrow
I'll hold a rifle in my hand
Eighteen yesterday........ my birthday
Hope I live to be a man

Can I do it?
You bet I can
Semper Fi
God Bless Them Everyone
Written by
Bonnie Ray and Maryfrances Perez

Angels On The Hill

In the arms of the angels they flew away
A hot wind blowing across the desert
on that fateful day
<><><><><><><>
Those so brave who fought and died
from their fate they did not hide
These so young and brave
are warriors still
<><><><><><><>
Tonight they'll stand their watch
from heaven's hill
<><><><><><><>
Far above the battlefield
they'll be their brother's warrior shield
<><><><><><><>
In the arms of the angels they flew away
yet their spirit is in the hearts of those
that fight on today
<><><><><><><>
Their red road has come to it's end
Yet their warrior hearts beat
in our young women and men
written by Bonnie Ray
And Ernie Smiling Hawk

Bonnie Ray

Portrait Of A Mother

The bravest battle that was ever fought,
Shall I tell you where and when?
On the maps of the world you'll find it not
'Twas fought by the mothers of men.

Nay, not with cannon or battle shot,
With swords or noble pen,
Nay, not with the eloquent word or thought,
From the mouths of wonderful men.

But deep in the walled-up woman's heart
Of women that would not yield.
But, bravely, silently bore their part
Lo, there is the battlefield.

No marshaling troops, no bivouac song,
No banner to gleam and wave;
But oh, these battles they last so long
From babyhood to the grave.

The above poem was found in an old Baptist church
bible dated 1967-Author Unknown
This was given to me by a friend to share
Thank you R.Brent

Visions Of Grandfather

I could only see a part of his face
A feathered bonnet shadowed
His cheeks and chin
His eyes sparkling and
The face ..dark upward.. without a grin
He seemed... to be speaking to me
But I could only hear a mournful sound
Then I knew...... Grandfather was praying
With his hands high and kneeling on the ground
I have seen you...
Many times before... My Grandfather
On this same mountain, In your evening prayer calls
And then my vision faded ..leaving echos of the past.
As I remembered....
His love and words of wisdom on my recalls
R,Brent & Bonnie Ray

Bonnie Ray

Spirit Fathers

When I was hungry
You quenched my thirst
With bountiful knowledge
Of mother earth
When I was naked you taught me
About clothing and shelter
From the storms of life
When I was ill
You comforted me and my dire need
And taught me to be humble
And aware of mans open greed
When I was lonesome
You never left me alone
Our prairies were together in
Lifes dream and song
Only now I see the wisdom
Of great ones gone on before
Vivid and clear..seems like
Their lives reflect to me
Like a flashing mirror
From an open door
Written by R.Brent
    and Bonnie Ray

Cherokee Evening Prayer

I have a great spirit up on high
Who has for me a fathers care
An eternal grace stretches wide
Over all my skies he abides
Often may the want... of faith
The question brings....
Not to forsake me...
In lifes eternal ring
I seem plagued by sorrow..
And surrounded by worldly sin
Upon a wild sea in this world
We go astray within
I am calling upon his grace
For me to be found
Listening for....
The great spirits calling
At the door of my heart

Are you still around ?

Native Americans
Cherokee

B.Ray & R. Brent

Bonnie Ray

Childhoods Summer Rain

After a long day working in the hot summer sun
The shadows of clouds and a stillness would come
The sound of distant thunder with lightning all around
We as a family would wait for the cool dampening rain
To touch the ground...as gathered from many we
Came..and all became one..a true bonding once again we
Found...was it a cast
Those days are now...so many years past.
Only treasured memories in my mind still last.
So when I sit all alone and watch a rainstorm on my
porch
I so vividly recall...some of the best days of my youth
When family was considered paramount and enjoyed by
all
A treasured memory can make you smile ..when nothing
else can
Be humble and recall... all the good times when you can
For if a rain can bring you memories...
It could just be....God and natures plan
Rick Brent 4/24/01
Dedicated to Bonnie Ray

Grandpa's Note

Grandpa always said
Next day for tomorrow's
First day in the rest of your life
Yesterday is past
Tomorrow is a present....a gift
But he who damns today
And lives for tomorrow
Is philosopher in fools advice
And vice versa
Life is too short and too sweet

To withstand to much pain or sorrow
You may be here today
And gone tomorrow
So after all is said and done
Only the truth will hold
This will create a free spirit
Peace and contentment to behold
R.B.-B.R.

Bonnie Ray

Flowers Of Light

Ask the flowers in the valley
Oh where are you facing too
They will answer....toward the sun
There is where I get my glow
Flowers are just like souls
They turn toward the light
They bend toward it..
With all their might
In the shadows they humbly
Cover their bloom.
And with the morning light
Again rebloom
-R. Brent & Bonnie Ray

Journey Of The Hummingbird

One of the most beautiful and fragile fowls,we all love
and know id the Hummingbird
Like a delicate flower lives for the summer,
and will die in the snow
They migrate south at summers long end
Such a long and tiring journey
they hitch a ride with a feathered friend
Nestled under a drakes wing
dep inside it's down
The small hummingbird is safe on it's long flight
high above the ground
This journey could take weeks to complete
and from the drakes life blood it must drink
The journey for survival had for both started too late
From lack of nourishment and weakened   by the ducks
blood flow, at journeys near end, they both tumbled
to the ground,and were found dead in the cold winter
snow.
These beautiful fowl creatures.. lives extinguished !
Only one of natures tragic songs.
We all wait much too long, before acting upon life's
journey
and we are left cold and alone.
R. Brent --Bonnie Ray

Bonnie Ray

Sunsets Kiss

Watching sunsets descent in my evening sky all aglow
The array of colors enhance the Western Sky
While the wildflowers wait arow
As the kiss of dew falls
Upon the fragrant sweet grass talls
To quench away the thirst of day
Sunsets reflection upon the streams mirrored glass
Gentle evening song of sound begins
Chanting a melody that lasts
Another day soon to pass
While I in slumber rest
And wait for tomorrows renewed repast

-R. Brent &Bonnie Ray

Life Preparation

Our culture does not prepare for death
We exempt it as part of our lives
Regradless of our age and training
We all think alike
Life is a preparation of death
And what we do in between
Is our legacy left behind to others
Our lives must flow like an open stream
And when our final curtain is drawn
And life is at end
If not prepared for the inevitable
This is man's greatest sin
Walk your path and do
With what you have gained
and been given
The Great Spirit
knows he the one to whom
His Grace is given

R.Brent B.Ray

Bonnie Ray

Book Of Life

Within the book of our life,
are pages filled with many things.
Some are written by strife
While others are written by love

Upon each page a story told
Some sad ones, glad ones,
and some are written in gold

As the years go by, and each chapter ends
there comes a page written,
remembering loved ones and friends,
where we shared love, laughter,
heartaches and tears.

Another page written
by the passing of years
Then one of lessons learned
as our wisdom's we earned

Before the last chapter is written,
we hope that when the book is read,
what we leave behind for others to see...
is a life lived fully and not one misread...

Filled with love and good meaning

remembered by all..
As one..that was worth reading

Co-written by
Bonnie Ray And Rick Brent

Bonnie Ray

Spirited Eagles Family Love

Listen closely when
On a hill or valley low
The cry of an eagle..
Calling for his love
This you can plainly hear.
His soul torrents of a melody
Pouring out on his shadow below
And it glistens and refracts
Upon the cold winters snow
Brave and not feeling imperiled
He searches the countryside alone
On an empty flight.
He searches for food a loving gift
For his family on a cold evening
And oncoming night
Thinking of his family not self
More than others may be
And with family pride
And proud to be an eagle
Knows God created he
The loving thoughts never vanish
His homeward flight and driving spirit
Pushes him on..the love
Of his waiting family
Prompted his open heart
When he arrives home

His love with family to be shared
He has one of Gods greatest gifts
Of love sharing he is loved
And is Gods own

R.Brent B.Ray

Chapter Ten

The following poems are to heighten the awareness to the crimes committed against our children. Everyday an innocent child is molested and a life is left in sorrow . We must all be aware and protect our children. If you suspect child abuse or molestation do not hesitate to investigate.

Even Little Hearts Bleed

Does anybody hear me? Does anybody care?
Does anybody hear my screams? Is anybody there?
This door is locked. I don't know why.
I promised I would never tell, I wouldn't even cry
I am your child. You watch me bleed...
All you think of is this sick need.

What did I do to deserve this pain?
You leave no marks but scars remain.
Deep inside where no one knows
A spirit dies; Only fear now grows
.

Yet you call Me the demon seed;
You'll never see even little hearts bleed.
You look at me and see no love;
You hated me from the day I was born.
So unwanted and so very unloved

You beat my body with your cruel words.
I cry myself to sleep at night;
No one tells me stories or holds me tight.
You use me for your pleasure and leave me;
I hug my pillow tight for comfort all night
You say you love me, yet you hurt me so
I will promise not to tell a soul.
Is this some curse, a strange new disease?

I was not the first, oh God help me please!
I will do what you say even though it does not feel right;
Please just leave me alone, Let me rest tonight.

I hear your footsteps outside my door
You are coming for me, once more
Why can't God .....stop you dead?
I Pray that I could die
As you stand there beside my bed
Someday please,.... someone hear my pleas...
by Maryfrances, Myrna D. Badgerow, Floreann,
Tom Atterberry, and Bonnie Ray
© 2002 All Rights Reserved

A Note From The Heart Of The Poets

If you suspect any type of child abuse have the
heart and the courage to make your concerns known.
A child may someday thank you....

1-800-252-2873 Child Abuse Hotline

Stop The Hatred

We are suffering in body and spirit
As we remember times past
Pain of war and killing
A great sorrow surrounding so many
Needless inhuman acts on the innocent
Such hate and such great fear
Creating pain as bitter tears fall
Nothing left of those who lived
A pile of shoes all tattered and worn
Hearts crushed and bodies torn.

The crying echoes through the night
Carried by the wind
Forever we must pay the price
For all of those who've sinned
Hold your brother to your heart
Help to ease his pain
Without your strength to lean on
His sorrow will remain
Hate is legislated in the heart
And can fill your soul with bile
Hold on to your sister's hand
Help her walk that mile
Prejudice, anger, hatred and greed
These are all fruit from the demon seed

Find acceptance in your heart
Forgiveness brings a brand new start.

Must we go on until we see
Oceans of blood and inhumanity
Do so many lust for mans mortal end
That we cannot come together
And revaluate the meaning of brotherhood or friend
Can we not just lay down our weapons
And make a way to understand
Before we destroy this planet
And then where will the mighty victor stand?

Many lives were given to protect
The goodness God gave this land
And as Children of God
We will take you by the hand
Meet us in love and peace
We will never let freedom cease
United we shall win against evils sin
With love and peace we welcome you in
In war and hatred , there is no win.
Stop The Hatred"
by Floreann Cawley, Maryfrances Perez
Tom Atterberry, and Bonnie Ray

*This author is one that gives you her heart and soul
in one book. A gift to all that read her and are lucky
enough to buy or give this book as a gift. For it is truly
a book of all seasons and times. A keepsake that gives a
lifetime of enjoyment to those that enjoy poetry .*

Bonnie Ray

Cherokee Blessing

May the warm winds of heaven
blow softly upon your house
May the Great Spirit
Bless all who enter there
May your moccasins make
happy tracks in many snows
And may the rainbows
always touch your shoulder
May you walk in peace love and harmony

Printed in the United Kingdom
by Lightning Source UK Ltd.
104734UKS00001B/211